Everyday Etiquette

EVERYDAY ETIQUETTE

Grace Fox

A ROUNDTABLE PRESS BOOK

GUILDAMERICA BOOKS®

DOUBLEDAY DIRECT, INC.

GARDEN CITY, NEW YORK

Contents

	INTRODUCTION	7
1.	FAMILY LIFE	9
2.	SINGLE LIFE	40
3.	FRIENDSHIPS	63
4.	OFFICE LIFE	85
5.	PUBLIC LIFE	108
6.	ENTERTAINING	135
7.	TABLE MANNERS	175
8.	CORRESPONDENCE AND PROTOCOL	202
9.	CEREMONIES	228
10.	LOSSES	254
	APPENDIX 1: BIRTHSTONES	279
	APPENDIX 2: TRADITIONAL ANNIVERSARY GIFTS	280
	INDEX	282

Introduction

MANNERS ARE AN INVALUABLE TOOL FOR GETTING ALONG with other people. Too often, though, we let them scare us. We pretend that they are too formal or prissy for our daily lives. This is because we think manners are really about knowing which fork to use or writing thank-you notes—what my mother calls watching your p's and q's.

On a certain level, of course, this is exactly what they are all about, a set of rather specific rules. But if we look deeper, we will see the real function of manners is to enable us to get along better with one another. They are about treating others as we ourselves would like to be treated, so that in return we will be treated well.

It is not so much that we must know which fork to use (and no truly well-mannered person would ever look down on someone for not using the right fork) as it is that we all believe eating will be a more enjoyable experience if we agree to use a fork. And ultimately life itself will be more pleasant if we agree to follow certain social conventions.

Other forms such as writing a thank-you note serve an even more sophisticated purpose. When we encourage, inspire, applaud, commend, congratulate, or otherwise support our fellow humans, we give people something that we hope eventually to get back. Naturally this anticipated payback should not be our only motivation, but it is a powerful force that helps to make the world—especially our immediate world—function more smoothly.

In this book you will learn how to use several kinds of forks and how and when to write a thank-you note (as well as other kinds of notes), *and* you will learn the kind of essential consideration that eases the way in our interactions with one another. You will learn, in short, how to move through life with confidence and grace. This is what manners are truly all about.

Chapter 1

FAMILY LIFE

MANY PEOPLE DON'T THINK OF HOME AS A PLACE THAT demands our best behavior, and it's true that this is where we're allowed to relax and be ourselves. But it's also true that home is where we nurture one another and build the strength and confidence necessary to cope successfully with the outside world. And etiquette, which is, after all, how we behave toward one another, can help us do this.

THE HARMONIOUS MARRIAGE

It is often in the small courtesies couples show to one another that they reveal the real strength of their relationship. Good manners can't make up for a bad marriage, but they can make a good one even better.

Naturally no couple gets along all the time, and each of us must make compromises to live with one another. And when we are unhappy, we must air our grievances. Manners should never be used to cover up problems, but they can help us discuss our problems fairly. Good manners also help to keep a marriage alive and exciting. Here are some tips that will help you do this:

• Disagree fairly. When you do air complaints, do so kindly. Always acknowledge the other person's point of view, even when you disagree with it. Saying things such as "You are right about that" and "I didn't know you felt that way" help you do this. If you are wrong, be quick to apologize, and do it in a loving way.

• When you do disagree, don't do it in public. Husbands and wives owe each other a basic level of courtesy and even a certain degree of protection when they are in public. Therefore when you disagree about something, take it home and discuss it privately. One partner should never yell or speak disagreeably to another in public.

• Don't use a public occasion—like a dinner party—as a forum to criticize your partner. I was once friends with a couple who did this. The husband would ask an innocent question such as "What do you think about couples who maintain separate checking accounts?" and as soon as I finished my answer, I would realize we weren't discussing social trends: we were talking about their relationship, and he was determined to complain about his wife with me as the referee. It's not fair to your partner—and it's definitely not fair to your friends.

• Be discreet. Couples owe each other this above all else. When talking to friends, never reveal any intimate details about your partner that would embarrass him.

• Speak well of one another. We all complain about the opposite sex on occasion, and there's nothing wrong with that, but it is another thing to denigrate your partner on a personal level. Don't do it. It makes you look bad, and it embarrasses those to whom you are speaking. If you have a complaint about your spouse, take it up with her directly.

- Look good for each other. For most of us, the days are gone when a wife changed clothes every evening so she could look extra spiffy greeting her husband. But you do owe it to your partner, whether you are a man or a woman, to stay fit and healthy and to look as attractive as you can.

- Make some time for each other every day. With our busy lives, this is easier said than done. But do try to set aside a few minutes each day to catch up with one another.

- Maintain a joint social calendar. This means you don't make dates without consulting one another. If someone invites you somewhere, it's acceptable and polite to reply that you must first check with your wife or husband.

- Use "we" and "our" often. We've all known a man who speaks of "my boat" or the woman who talks about "my house." Once, I even heard a man refer to his wife's "wastebasket" when showing off *their* new kitchen. This isn't mere semantics. The couple who speaks as if they are a team usually are one. It's that simple.

- Respect one another's privacy. However much you are a "we," you are also still individuals, and that means each of you is entitled to whatever measure of privacy you need or want. Each couple must work out what this means for them, but a good starting place is to not read one another's mail or browse through your partner's dresser drawers, boxes, or other special storage places. It is inexcusable to read your mate's diary or journal, even if it is left open in plain view.

- Help one another. One partner should not sit idly by and watch the other partner work. Even if the husband loves cooking dinner and knows that his wife will do the cleanup, he still appreciates an offer to help. If you have assigned duties, then it may be okay for one partner to stand by doing nothing while the other partner works, but even when certain tasks are assigned, most partners still appreciate the occasional helping hand.

• Do your share. Especially when both partners work outside the home, no one person should shoulder the burden of maintaining the household. If you have agreed to do specific chores around the house, do them. Without complaint.

• Ask for help when you need it. Martyrdom is not a pleasant trait, and it seems to thrive more in marriages than in any other kind of relationship. Even if you and your partner have carefully divided the work load, you may occasionally find yourself in a pinch and need some extra help. When this happens, don't sulk, ask for help.

• Say "Please" and "Thank you." It's absolutely amazing how much mileage you can get out of these three words.

A Couple's Social Life

Now that we are marrying later, most of us bring an array of old friends into a marriage, and we strive to make new friends—both married and single—as well. One of the ongoing tasks of any marriage is the sorting out of these friendships and the carving out of a social life that is pleasant for both partners.

Luckily, couples no longer always socialize together, something that was expected of them even twenty years ago. Today's practice of socializing both singly and as a couple is easier on both friendships and marriages. It also leaves you with several options for dealing with people whom one of you doesn't particularly care for.

One partner can see the friend alone all the time, although this may eventually arouse suspicion. Better still is to see the friend alone most of the time and bring your partner along now and then. (Sometimes old friends strive to spend some time alone, and doing so doesn't indicate any level of disharmony with the absent partner.) Unfortunately, if you can't work out something along these lines, then the de facto solution is to see less of the friend, which seems unkind if you truly treasure the friendship. In this instance your spouse may agree to see someone she doesn't particularly care for as a special favor to you. It's a favor, though, that shouldn't be asked too often—and one that should be warmly rewarded.

Domestic Affairs

Today the majority of couples share responsibilities at home. Yet however common sharing now is, it remains a bone of contention in many homes, mostly because couples don't know how to use diplomacy and tact in dealing with one another. The trouble lies not in what we ask of one another, but in how we ask.

Good manners go a long way when you're negotiating the division of labor. For one thing, ask, don't command. You'll always get farther phrasing a request in tactful terms, such as "Would you mind cleaning out the front hall closet?" or "Would you please rake the leaves?" rather than the more belligerent "You said you'd clean that closet three weeks ago. When are you going to do it?"

Putting the shoe on the other foot, if you can't deliver on an assigned chore, renegotiate another time to do it or politely ask your spouse to take over your chore temporarily. Above all else, say you're sorry you can't carry your load.

Particularly around the area of domestic chores, good manners often get lost early. It starts when we either forget or simply stop complimenting our mates for doing their share. Then we somehow stop asking and start commanding.

So the next time you find yourself about to tell your partner to do something, take a deep breath and say instead: "Would you mind . . . ?"

Money Doesn't Talk

Nowhere do loyalty and discretion come into play more than where family finances are involved. The urge to keep up with the Joneses may be universal, but your family's financial situation—or, for that matter, your friendship with the Joneses—won't be helped one bit if you reveal too much about this aspect of your life.

As a single person the decision to share your financial life with friends is far simpler than when you are married. When there are two of you, you no longer have the right to reveal such intimate details of your life to others—unless, of course, you and your partner agree that this is acceptable. If you don't, then your salaries, your investments, and especially your financial difficulties are off limits to friends and, for that matter, even to family members.

FAMILY LIFE WITH CHILDREN

Children obviously change the dynamic of family life in many ways. The cozy relationship you've worked out with your partner now must be rethought, and while there are added rewards, there are also added pressures. Manners can often be very helpful in sorting out what you owe one another in your new roles.

Living with a Baby

The first few months with a new baby are stressful for any marriage. No one except the baby is getting enough sleep, and almost every carefully established routine is thrown into disarray. For many couples, the reservoir of good feeling that has built up over the years often dribbles away.

Most helpful is to be aware of what is happening and to do whatever possible to salvage the situation. It's a time to be particularly sensitive to your own and your partner's needs. And since those needs may have changed dramatically since you brought the little one home, it's also a time to speak up about your needs and perhaps even to renegotiate. If you want your partner to spell you for a few hours so you can have some time to yourself, say so. It can be hard for others to guess what you need.

Every new set of parents has to decide what works best, but that veneer of manners, which after all is nothing more than treating each other kindly, is a definite help in getting through this wonderful and trying period.

Children's Manners

Apart from helping and supporting each other as you parent, teaching your children manners is another important task of parenting. This process can begin as soon as children are old enough to speak. The crux of manners is to teach your children to respect others, but before they can master this, they must feel respected themselves. There are several ways to show respect toward a small child.

- Ask your child what she wants rather than deciding for her. Obviously you'll make most of the decisions, but some can still be left even to a small child. You can ask whether she would like a peanut-butter sandwich or a yogurt for lunch or whether she would like to wear the red or the blue dress.

- Respect your child's privacy. Like adults, children

need their space and their privacy. The Golden Rule works well here. If you don't want your children barging in on you (a major complaint of many parents), then don't barge in on them. Knocking at the door of a child's room before entering is an effective way to teach him that you expect the same treatment in return.

• Be polite yourself. Without fail, one of the best and easiest ways to teach small children manners is to display them yourself. If they hear you saying "thank you" and "please" as you go through the day, they will learn to do the same. If they hear you and your partner really listening to each other, and observe that you treat one another kindly and generously, they will learn to do this as well.

As a child grows up, she needs to learn—and practice—social skills. It's best to start with simple skills, such as saying "please" and "thank you." Then move on to more complex issues such as sharing toys, not interrupting conversations, and greeting and shaking hands with visitors.

When possible, rehearse new behaviors with your child before he is expected to use them. For example, if you're teaching your child how to shake hands or say hello to adults, then practice doing this before a visitor comes to your home.

As your child learns manners, be patient. Don't forget we all learn through repetition. Don't expect to tell your child once not to interrupt you and have her understand this. Repeat your request not to be interrupted as needed.

And if your child balks at the last moment, don't press. Children take great pride in doing these things, but they sometimes like to choose the moment.

By the time a child is four or five, he is usually ready for some of the more advanced rituals of our society. Before a child's birthday party, for example, he could be taught how to make people feel welcome, as well as how to thank them for bringing a present. A child of this age is also old enough to understand that gifts should be opened slowly and displayed to the guests.

As your child masters each level of skills, move on to more advanced ones, such as thank-you notes and even table manners, which are perhaps the most complex manners we all must master.

Teaching Table Manners

Don't try to teach table manners before your child is old enough to handle them. The average three-year-old doesn't have the physical coordination to eat with a knife and fork, but by the time your child is four or five you can begin to suggest "nicer" ways of eating. (For suggestions on how to eat, see Chapter 7, Table Manners.)

An especially enjoyable way to teach your child table manners is to plan a special family dinner or a nice dinner in a restaurant. Before the event, discuss what you'll expect in the way of specific behavior. You may even want to stage a brief dress rehearsal.

Make the event as fun as possible. Perhaps let your child wear special dress-up clothes—or not, if that's what makes his heart go pitter-patter. Order a surprise dessert at the end of the meal. Include a special friend of your child's in the dinner party. (And his parents should be eternally grateful if some of this rubs off on their child.) If you make learning good table manners a pleasant and rewarding experience, your child will take to them easily and will display great pride in using them.

Teaching Children to Share

Perhaps the most important lifelong and lasting trait you can instill in your children is the ability to share with others.

Children begin to learn generosity around age three or four when you encourage them to share toys with their friends and siblings. As they get older, one hopes they will learn to share not only material possessions, but also themselves, their time, education, and skills.

Teaching Children to Use Titles

In many circles, children call adults—all and any adults—by their first names. In just as many circles, though, children do not do this, and the custom of calling friends' parents "Mr. Nelson" or "Mrs. McCormick" still prevails in many parts of the country. I think it is extremely courteous when parents teach their children to use titles and surnames with adults, but I can also recognize how awkward it is for a child to be made to march to a different drumbeat. Therefore, it is understandable when parents bow to this informality even though they might prefer not to.

Children's Correspondence

Even in this era of instant communication, some occasions call for a thank-you note, and as soon as children are old enough to write, they should be taught to write their own thank-you notes.

To make the experience pleasant, consider ordering special stationery for your child to use. Most stationers these days carry a line of brightly colored, lively writing papers just for children. An even bigger thrill is having their name printed on it. And even if you don't feel like custom-ordering stationery, you can buy less expensive paper designed especially for children.

By the way, until your child is old enough to write his own thank-you notes, the task falls to you. I recommend using your own stationery and writing in your own voice. I suspect I'm not alone in disliking the currently popular custom whereby parents write thank-you notes in a child's voice. I think most of us would rather receive a real thank-you from an adult than a fake one from a child.

Another problem that comes up these days is what, if anything, grandparents and others should do when they don't receive thank-you notes. It is very frustrating for someone who has spent time and energy picking out a child's gift to hear not a word about how it was received.

One grandmother told me that she fired off notes to each of her delinquent grandchildren, expressing and describing her dismay over not hearing from them in this situation. She told them they had received their last gift from her unless she started getting thank-you notes from them.

This was a fair way to handle the situation. First, she took up the issue with the children, not with their parents. Second, she gave warning. And third, she explained why she was doing this. When I bumped into her a few months later, I asked what results she had gotten, and she smiled and said she now gets prompt thank-you notes.

Living With Teenagers

By the time your children are teenagers, they need more from you in the way of respect, and you in turn should be able to expect more of them.

Teens generally like their privacy, and a savvy and polite parent should have no trouble complying with this. They also need more autonomy, and while this may not sound like a topic for an etiquette book, that autonomy can be given grudgingly or graciously.

For their part, teenagers should be capable of making introductions (see page 67 for details). They should be able to entertain adults graciously in your absence, settling them onto a comfortable chair and serving them a beverage. For that matter, they should be able to carry on a conversation with adults. Then again, these days I too often find that the problem is not getting teens to talk to adults, but getting them to stop. Parents should remember (and remind their teens) that they are not adults and thus should not dominate adult conversations.

Teens should show respect to people older than they by standing to greet them, shaking hands, letting them pass through doors first (and holding the door open for them), and offering to help them with small packages or chores.

Although I don't imagine there's a parent alive who doesn't have to do a lot of refereeing, teenagers are old enough to begin to respect their siblings' feelings and property. It's up to parents, though, to draw some lines. The best approach is to have a few simple and relatively rigid rules about these matters. For example, you might insist that your older children not take one another's possessions without asking permission. Or you might insist that they not enter a sibling's room without an invitation. The lines you need to draw will depend to a large extent on how well your children get along with each other.

When your children do perform well socially, be sure to compliment them warmly. If you return home late for a meeting and find that your teen has indeed settled in your guests, offered them beverages, and otherwise acted the role of host in your absence, be profuse in your thanks. Thank him right away in the presence of your guests, but it's a nice fillip to mention his good work several more times over the next few days just to let him know how really proud you are.

Youthful Friendships

When your children are old enough to have friends, they should be able to entertain them at home. You can and should set limits about when guests can visit, but let your children invite their friends home as soon as they are able to do so. As much as possible, let your child issue her own invitations and take the initiative in planning any activities.

Older children also should learn to be supportive and sympathetic to their friends. If your son's friend's parents separate or divorce, it will be a topic of conversation in your home. And while you're allaying your child's anxieties about his own domestic life, you can also discuss with him what he might do to be supportive of his friend.

In fact, one of the best things you can do for your children is to be on the alert for ways to instill in them genuine caring and sensitivity.

Adult Children Returning to the Nest

One of the more trying—and also more common—situations that arise among families today is the return of an adult child, who lives at home for a brief period until he is ready to move into his own home. It's difficult on several levels, but mostly because everyone has gotten used to having things their way and, however much parents and child may love each other, they may find it difficult to readjust to the new living arrangements, especially if they become long term.

Many questions arise: Who does the laundry? Does the returning child pay for the food she eats? And of course the big one: Can lovers spend the night? Obviously manners can't solve all the problems connected to this situation, but they can help.

To tackle the most difficult question first: An adult child returning to his parents' house is expected to abide by their wishes, within reason. This means that if your parents disapprove of overnight guests with whom you are intimate, you should arrange to stay together elsewhere. Parents cannot stop you from spending the night away from home, but it is a courtesy to let them know when you will not be coming home, although you need not provide details of your whereabouts.

As for the more nitty-gritty details of daily living, an adult living with her parents should do as much of her maintenance as she would were she living on her own. She should make a special effort to keep the house, especially the bathroom, as tidy and clean as if she were not living there. Whatever parents do for an adult child in the way of cleaning, cooking, and other forms of maintenance should be viewed as a favor, not an obligation, and treated accordingly. It is especially gracious for the adult child to buy her parents an occasional dinner out or some other gift or treat as a gesture of thanks.

As for the question of paying rent, it is certainly appropriate to expect an adult child to contribute something to a household, but many parents are not comfortable asking for this, which in turn creates an unspoken tension. It's better by far for the family to sit down together and, as kindly and tactfully as possible, discuss these issues right at the start of the living arrangement instead of letting them smolder. All sides must be given room to air their views. If you aren't going to charge your child but you would like to, this should be discussed, and if you do plan to ask for money, you should explain your reasons for doing so. Finally, an adult child who is asked to pay some household expenses should acquiesce to the request graciously even if he does not believe this is an appropriate thing to do.

Turf Wars and Other Not-So-Minor Problems of Family Life

Most of the day-to-day family problems boil down to turf wars—skirmishes over the things we share, most notably the telephone, the television, and the bathroom.

Telephone Etiquette

When you live with other people, you are their answering service, like it or not. And the telephone is a shared instrument in most homes. Here are a few rules to reduce the friction:

• Don't hog the telephone. If you do need your monthly hour-long conference with an old friend, try to arrange it when you're home alone or at a time when others are unlikely to want the phone.

• Be aware of others' needs. If your partner is expecting a call, hold back on any calls you have to make if you can.

• Answer other family members' calls politely, especially if you want the same from them.

• Take messages carefully. Write them down, then repeat any information or telephone numbers to the caller so you're sure to get the message right. If you use an answering machine, decide whether you'll take notes or save the message so the person for whom it's intended can hear it.

• Don't let very small children answer the phone. Mostly this is for the convenience of those who call you. It's a real nuisance to be kept dangling by an incoherent three-year-old.

• Don't assume your friends want to talk to your children. Usually just when we're most rushed, a friend will ask if we want to speak to little Joanie, aged two and not nearly as precocious as her parents would like to believe. It's up to parents to be sensitive to this situation and keep their small children away from the phone.

TV Etiquette

We all know what this boils down to: channel surfing and who gets to watch what. This is an area for polite negotiation. For example, while it's okay to ask your surfer to stop, it's an even bigger act of kindness to wait a few minutes before you make your request. And as for program viewing, we're fortunate these days in that most VCRs allow divided households to watch one show and tape another.

Bathroom Manners

Lots of stress and bad feeling could be avoided if every person had his own bathroom, but alas, few of us are so lucky. In the absence of this luxury, here are a few tips on sharing:

• Don't monopolize the bathroom. You have no choice but to take turns. When you do plan to take a nice long bath, reserve the room in advance and let everyone know beforehand that you plan to be in there for a while.

• Always knock before entering a bathroom to be sure it's unoccupied.

• Clean up the sink or bathtub after use, replace the cap on the toothpaste, and otherwise leave things in good order for the next person.

• Don't use all the hot water. In most houses there is a finite amount. It's unpleasant for everyone if one person runs down the supply.

Building Traditions

One of the most important purposes of family life is to build traditions. We do this by celebrating occasions such as anniversaries and birthdays, by keeping holidays that have special meaning for us, and by creating special occasions of our own.

One family I know regularly schedules their own version of musical and literary evenings. The evening always has a theme—favorite childhood books was one and scary ghost stories another. I was fortunate enough to be invited to a sixties rock music evening, where the parents sought (unsuccessfully, I must admit) to induct their heavy-metal-oriented teenagers into the world of Janis Joplin and the Beatles. Still, a very good time was had by all, and I can't help but think these evenings will live on in the warm memories of those who participate in them.

Another family, whose members (like most of us) live scattered and separate lives during the week, always have Saturday brunch together; they can make plans at any other time except for these few special hours. On Saturday morning they use cloth napkins, pretty dishes, glasses, and flatware—and enjoy a long, leisurely meal that's full of jokes and catching up on the week. Not so coincidentally, meals like these are also a way to teach your children—in a light, unpressured setting—how to live graciously and, even more important, how to enjoy the smaller moments of life.

It's important to take time to celebrate the big, traditional holidays as well—occasions when everyone can be together to participate in special family rituals and traditions, whatever they are.

IN-LAWS/OUT-LAWS

One of the touchier aspects of family life, for many people, anyway, is in-law relations. They may be family, but they're not, well, *your* family. Still, there are several things you can do to keep relations congenial.

Calling Each Other Names

Names are a minor but sometimes significant source of discord in many families. Your mother-in-law wants to be called "Mother," and you're not comfortable with this. You want to retain your maiden name, and your mother-in-law isn't comfortable with that.

To start, try to negotiate to call your in-laws the name you want, which for most of us is a first name. Mothers-in-law, take note, it is up to you as the senior person in the relationship to initiate the discussion. But the daughter-in-law can, as was mentioned, negotiate.

If your mother-in-law asks you to call her "Mother," be tactful but honest. Tell her that while you love her very much, you don't think you'll ever be comfortable calling anyone but your own mother that, and is there anything else she would like? At this point a smart mother-in-law ought to take the hint and suggest that you settle on her first name.

Most families, unfortunately, never get around to a discussion like this. They opt for the cowardly way out, which is to call the in-laws nothing. This persists until children enter the picture, at which point the parents switch to "Grandma" and "Grandpa," which if any parents-in-law thought about for long is an even greater insult. What fifty-year-old wants a twenty-five-year-old calling her Grandma?

The name game also goes two ways now that many young

women keep their names when they marry—and many mothers-in-law (to say nothing of one's own mother, miscellaneous aunts, and other relatives) don't get it or don't approve.

How you handle this situation obviously depends upon how strongly you feel about fighting the good fight. When you do decide to correct someone, do so with a smile and pleasant tone. Also consider whether the person really didn't know—or remember—that you kept your maiden name or whether they didn't want to remember. Sometimes when the protest is political, the savviest—and least provocative—thing you can do is ignore it.

Merging Styles and Traditions

An overriding problem for many couples is how to merge their families' two styles, two sets of traditions, two ideas, of how things should be done. The Golden Rule works wonderfully well in this situation. From your point of view, this means that you do have a right to do things the way you want to in your own home. But don't forget the flip side is that others can do things they want in their own homes, and they should do this without criticism from you.

In even the closest family, people need to draw lines about what they will and won't tolerate. But as you spend more time together and get to know each other better, the lines will become easier to deal with. You'll understand what each of you wants, and you can begin to oblige one another your peccadilloes and eccentricities.

As for those traditions you don't share with your partner's family, flexibility goes a long way. Why not be open to new customs and traditions? If you know that a food or custom is particularly meaningful to your in-laws, try to incorporate it into your family's customs. So what if your family always finishes Christmas Eve dinner by eating a German chocolate cake? Wouldn't it be fun to add napoleons as well?

Most in-law relationships start with considerable goodwill and then deteriorate somewhat before settling down to a fairly amicable level. The key word here is amicable. We don't have to be best friends, but we do have to get along. We owe it to our spouses, and if everyone tries, it usually works.

THE INTERMARRIED FAMILY

Of course, when a couple is in a religious or racial intermarriage, the issues go deeper—and are harder to resolve. It helps to remember that your differences were part of what attracted you to one another, and they should therefore be relished as much after marriage as they were before.

Trickiest of all are those situations where children are involved. Once an intermarried couple has children, the drive for one's culture to dominate can come into play. While these issues often run deeper than mere etiquette, the compassion that underlies all manners can help you handle the situations that inevitably arise. One basic rule is to be as involved as possible in your partner's culture and religion. If your children attend religious services other than your own, for example, you should attend with them at least occasionally and participate as fully as you can. Similarly, if it is your religious services that your children attend, be sure to include your spouse as much as possible.

It also helps—and is enormously tactful—to acknowledge the culture and religion that does not dominate. I know a couple where the wife is Christian but her children are being reared in her husband's Jewish faith. Nevertheless, the man sensed his wife's loneliness and isolation at Christmas and has continued to have a Christmas tree even though they originally agreed not to have one once they had children. In fact, he has turned the selection of the tree into a family outing each year as he rounds up his family and heads for a Christmas tree farm where they can choose and cut down their own tree. He further uses the occasion to tell his children that they are doing this to honor Mom's holiday and to make her happy. Such large and small acts of compassion can go a long way toward soothing the wounded feelings that arise in such marriages. The Christmas tree is also a nice payback since many of the responsibilities for bringing up the children Jewish—taking them to Hebrew school, celebrating the holidays at home—fall on the wife.

Although most religions and many extended families like to see the children brought up in one religion to the total exclusion of the other, I feel this can be too divisive within the family, especially over the long term. It is, I think, kinder for the immediate family to make room for both cultures and religions, even when the children are formally being reared in one. Taking your Christian children, for example, to Dad's High Holiday services makes them more sophisticated about their own dual inheritance—and about the world at large.

When a Family Breaks Up

One of the saddest things that can happen to a family—and it happens frequently today—is divorce. Most of us aren't thinking about etiquette at such a time, but it can help us get past some of the rough patches.

Announcing the Breakup

It is never polite for others to ask what has happened, even if it's obvious your family has split up. They must wait until you decide to make an announcement, and there's no need for you to do this until you're ready. It's usually easiest to tell work colleagues and close friends first. If this is too painful, it's okay to ask a friend to let people know informally.

People you don't maintain regular contact with can be told in a brief note, preferably not the one you write on your annual holiday card. But if, like most of us, you use the cards to keep distant friends up on your news, and if this is your news, and you're unlikely to tell the friend any other way, then it's probably better to say something than nothing. Do think, though, about enclosing a separate note rather than writing it on the card. It is never appropriate to send any kind of formal announcement regarding the dissolution of a marriage. A name change may be formally announced, but no reason need be stated in the announcement.

When a friend or acquaintance announces that a marriage has broken up, the only polite response is, "I'm sorry." If your friend then wants to fill you in on how horrible his ex-wife was, you can offer more detailed sympathy, but until you know how your friend actually feels, don't say anything more. And if you feel that you're lying by saying "I'm sorry" to someone you know was married to an unpleasant person, remember that you aren't saying "I'm sorry you got rid of a lousy marriage partner" but, rather, "I'm sorry your marriage ended." It's a very rare person who doesn't feel the pain of the breakup, however relieved he may be to have the relationship ended.

Reconstituted Families

With divorce comes reconstituted families, which is what happens when people remarry and merge two families into one. Dealing with a reconstituted family is a little like dealing with in-laws. You all bring different ideas, attitudes, and traditions of family life into the relationship, and the problem becomes what to do with them all. As is the case with any family, though, common courtesy can get us through almost any situation.

- Treat everyone kindly. This means that even if your wife and her ex-husband are in the midst of a nasty spat, when he calls, you are cordial. If at all possible, don't let your bad feelings show, not least because any rudeness from you at this stage may well make matters worse for your wife.
- Make firm plans regarding the children. Many people wouldn't consider this a matter of good manners, but it very much is because it shows respect for others' time. It's rude (and maddening) to say, "We may want to take the kids apple picking this weekend." Either you will take them or you won't, and the other parent deserves firm, advance notice in order to make some plans.
- Be prompt. Other people have schedules to meet, times when they have to be somewhere, and they should be able to count on you. So when it's time to pick up the children, make sure you are there.
- Recognize what your responsibilities are and meet them. It's your job to pick up your kids when you say you will. If an emergency occurs and you can't, it's okay to ask your present spouse for help once in a while. But she has her set of responsibilities from her first marriage, and you have yours. It's kinder to one another to keep them separate.
- Do your share. Everything about a reconstituted family requires more work—doing the laundry, planning an outing, everything is more complicated because it involves more people. Therefore the best thing everyone can do is whatever is expected of them, whether it is the laundry or making a reservation for dinner. This is common courtesy to those around you.

- Stay out of what isn't your business. This is the hardest lesson to learn, perhaps, but the one with the most potential rewards once you master it. To a large extent, your husband is in charge of his children with his former wife, and you are in charge of yours. You are in charge of relations with your ex-spouse, and your husband is in charge of relations with his. Life gets sticky only when you meddle in other people's affairs, and things go more smoothly when you don't.

Finally, just as you learned to do with your in-laws, try to incorporate familiar traditions and customs from the other family into your own rituals. This serves the wonderful purpose of making everyone feel more at home.

HOUSEHOLD HELP

In 1900 a middle-class family in a city required a staff of seventeen to maintain itself. Today the average middle-class family considers itself lucky to have a cleaning woman, someone to care for the children while mom and dad work, and a baby-sitter for an occasional parents' night off.

In the early 1900s lines were carefully drawn between servants and employers. Servants wore uniforms and were deferential, and everyone agreed that a certain amount of distance helped maintain the employer-employee relationship. Today servants rarely wear uniforms (at least in middle-class households) and aren't necessarily deferential, and the lack of distance sometimes makes it impossible to tell who is the nanny and who is the mother. Even so, if you want to enjoy sound relations with those who work for you, it's important to know how to treat them—and how they should treat you, as well.

When someone works in your home, the work is supposed to be done on your terms, and it is absolutely appropriate and even expected that you will set the conditions, whether it's how you want your kitchen floor scrubbed or how you want your child talked to.

Having said this, however, I would quickly append that old cliché "You get more flies with honey than with vinegar." It's true: you'll always get more of what you want, with less wear and tear on you, if you treat those who work for you with kindness and respect. So here are a few guidelines for getting along with those who make your domestic life go more smoothly:

* Offer a stable work environment to whomever you hire. Explain the responsibilities that go along with the job as well as the salary and benefits. Then stick to them. This means that if you hired a cleaning woman for four hours and five rooms, then when you move, don't expect her to clean eight rooms in the same time and for the same money.

* Pay promptly. You hold someone's livelihood in your hands, and like you, that person must eat and pay rent. Establish when you will pay, and never fail to do so. No excuses are permitted, and that includes the fact that you didn't get to the bank or forgot to leave the money when you left for work in the morning. How would you feel if your child's caretaker forgot to take care of your child? It's amazing how often otherwise mannerly people think they can "borrow" from someone who works for them. And it always puts the employee in an awkward spot.

* Maintain a certain distance. Class distinctions truly have broken down, and there is no longer any reason to be as rigid as people were a hundred years ago, but the person who works for you is still your employee. This means you may have to offer criticism or, worse, end the relationship altogether, and in situations like this, a little distance goes a long way.

Hiring

An interview is an excellent place for both you and a prospective employee to show off your good manners. For starters, both of you should show up at the appointed time.

Remember when you ask difficult questions, and you must of course ask them, to do so as tactfully as possible, certainly without giving the appearance of grilling the person. For one thing, if you don't put the other person on the defensive, you're likely to learn much more. And remember that some questions—regarding a person's race, religion, or marital status, for example—are illegal.

If you're hiring someone for a position where manners will be important, such as a child caretaker, make this known during the interview. You can say, "We've tried to teach Ginny good manners, and we'll expect you to help us with that." Your prospective employee's face will either light up with relief because she knows exactly what you mean, or she won't understand your request, in which case she's probably not the person to work for you.

Firing

It's always tough to fire someone, but it must be done on occasion. These days, both to protect yourself legally and to show consideration for your employee, there are a few procedures you should follow.

First, give warning before you let someone go. Be clear about what isn't being done properly, and give your employee time to correct the problem.

If the situation doesn't improve, then politely explain—face-to-face if possible—that things don't seem to be working out, and you'll have to sever the relationship. Offer two weeks' pay if possible and appropriate, but think twice about letting someone remain in your home for any period of time once you've announced your decision. Relationships usually deteriorate rather quickly at this stage.

Criticizing Employees

Often it's possible to save an employer-employee relationship before it deteriorates entirely. One way to do this is to make it known when someone who works for you isn't doing the job the way you want it done.

Some people accumulate a list and then sit down with an employee, while others favor on-the-spot correction. Whichever method you choose, try to offer something good at the same time that you deliver the bad news. For example, you might say, "Sally, you've done a wonderful job taking care of Julie, but we also agreed that you would do some housecleaning, and it's not getting done." Alternately, if your employee has fallen down for personal reasons, it sometimes helps to offer acknowledgment first, saying, "Mary-ann, I know you haven't felt well this week, but I asked you to pick up the photographs because I really needed them, and now I don't have them."

Finally, be open to what your employee says back, especially if he is valued. Perhaps there is a problem that needs to be ironed out.

The People Who Work for You

Here are a few more specific suggestions for getting along with the people who work for you:

Cleaning Person

The person who cleans your house knows the most intimate details of your life, and that may be your fault. Consider these few hints on getting along with the cleaning person and preserving your privacy:

- Clean up before she comes. Everyone jokes about this, but in truth cleaning people appreciate it. And more important, it makes their real work easier. Your cleaning person's job isn't to put away your clothes from yesterday (unless you've both made this part of the deal); it's to give your home a good overall cleaning. Make it easy to do this.
- Don't leave out personal items that you would find offensive if you were cleaning someone's home.

Child Caretaker

If the person works in your home:

- Outline the parameters of the job. Make sure the employee knows the procedures that must be followed and what you expect. For example, if you want light housekeeping, make it part of the initial bargain—don't add it later. If your child is the first priority, make that clear, too.
- Don't expect more than what you've agreed to initially. It's not okay to ask your child caretaker to stay three extra hours because you need to work late—and it's especially not okay to assume she'll do this. People who work for you have personal lives, and you should respect this.

If the person works at a day care center:

- Arrive at the expected time to pick up your child. It's true, no one will sell your child if you don't get there promptly, but someone will have to stay late and probably won't get paid for it, so it doesn't make for a very happy situation.

• Don't send a sick child to day care. Of course, this complicates your life enormously, but you wouldn't want others sending their sick child to school with yours, so extend the same courtesy yourself.

Baby-sitters

There is a difference between a baby-sitter and a child caretaker: the baby-sitter is often a teenager who needs your guidance. This may mean telling her the candy bar is for her but the shrimp is for the party you're giving the following night.

There will also be additional concerns for the baby-sitter's safety. Young women who are still living in their parents' home should be taken home by you personally, especially if the hour is late. And if she's a student, don't assume you have much room to renegotiate your arrival time back home. Tell her when you will return and then stick to the time.

Live-in Help

Certain standards should be met to assure the comfort of employees who live in your home. They should have their own bathroom and their own bedroom, preferably one large enough to have a comfortable sitting area. Either stock the room with a refrigerator or let them know they may use yours when they choose.

The bedroom should be comfortably furnished with a bed, a night table, an upholstered easy chair, possibly a side chair as well, a table, a clock, a radio and a television. The furnishings can be simple, but the room should be cheerful and light.

Raises, Tips, and Gifts

The first thing you need to know is that these are three distinct categories. People who work for you will expect a raise about once a year. Depending upon what you have negotiated with them, they may also expect a bonus. A bonus is *not* a gift; it is usually negotiated in advance and is part of the salary. A tip or gift is something extra that you give.

Tips and gifts are typically given at Christmas or Chanukah or at the New Year. (If, like many, you are especially strapped during the holidays, you can tip at another time of year. For example, a friend of mine has worked out an arrangement whereby she gives her cleaning woman a major gift on her birthday and then gives only a token gift at Christmas.)

A good rule of thumb for someone who works regularly in your home is a week's pay as either a bonus or a holiday gift. Try to assess whether your employee would prefer a gift or money. If you're really unsure, you can always divide between the two.

If you do decide in favor of a gift, make it something appropriate. You might give a scarf, for example, but you wouldn't give intimate apparel. Soaps, bath oils, perfume (if you know what the person wears), a book, or a compact disc are all acceptable.

If you're given a gift you don't care for and wish to pass it on to someone who works for you, that's fine, but you shouldn't give it as a gift. Similarly, cast-off clothes and household belongings, however welcome they may be to your employee, are not substitutes for gifts.

FAMILY LIFE HAS MANY PURPOSES; MUTUAL SUPPORT AND the nurturing of young and old alike are two that spring to mind. But another purpose that's often overlooked is the simple transmission of one's lifestyle. I'm not referring to teaching your children every little rule about napkin folding and fork placement, but, rather, to teaching them about living graciously and leisurely—at least on occasion. And in addition to using the big occasions to impart this, it's important to show your family each day that you love and respect them—and for that you need employ only everyday common manners.

Chapter 2

SINGLE LIFE

❊

LIVING WELL IS SOMETHING YOU OWE YOURSELF, REGARD-less of your stage of life. Never can you pamper yourself more than during the periods you're on your own, without any special obligations to others. Despite this, many singles don't think in terms of setting up a household designed to accommodate their own needs or for entertaining their friends. This chapter contains tips on living *very* graciously as a single, as well as hints on managing a single social life.

FEATHERING YOUR NEST

Too many singles don't bother to feather their own nests, perhaps because they're afraid to look too settled. But you owe it to yourself to create a comfortable, cozy environment, and you owe it to your friends to have a pleasant place to bring them to. And, yes, these days you are expected to entertain even though you're single.

You need not invest in major pieces of furniture or decorate in a lavish way, but you do need a functional household. Basically this means a comfortable living room, a well-stocked kitchen, and, for most people, some way of accommodating guests, either in a second bedroom or on a comfortable foldout sofa or a futon. Several major stores today specialize in "first apartment" furniture: inexpensive, often tasteful, and these days sophisticated enough to appeal to the older single as well.

One of the great advantages of buying inexpensive furniture is that you can experiment to find out what your style is. And of course, if you're seriously interested in good antiques or art, nothing should stop you from buying the best. The important thing is not to look as if you're living in a lifeboat, waiting for a larger ship to come along and save you. This discourages both friends and lovers.

ENTERTAINING

Just as singles aren't expected to feather their nests in the same way marrieds do, they also need not entertain on the same scale—but they are expected to do *some* entertaining. Everyone understands that many singles live in smaller houses or apartments than their married friends and family and thus may not be able to return invitations tit for tat, but this is no excuse for never making an effort.

Budget considerations can prohibit your planning a lavish dinner party that a two-income couple can easily afford, but you can do something more casual. If you're not interested in cooking and you eat out all the time anyway, you can always entertain in a restaurant.

The point is to entertain in any way that suits you, as long as you do something to pay back the invitations you have accepted throughout the year. You can even use one invitation to pay back several, especially if you have budget restrictions or prefer large parties to small ones. For example, one man I know throws a single huge holiday cocktail party to pay back all the invitations he's accepted throughout the year.

Especially good ways for singles with limited space and budgets to entertain are dessert and coffee, cookouts, cocktails, and simple buffet brunches, lunches, and dinners. Buffet meals can be pulled together easily. Cocktail parties are also making a comeback, and there is no easier way to entertain. (Hints on how to organize various parties can be found in Chapter 6.)

Getting Out and Meeting People

A big concern for many singles is how to go about building an active social life. This is sometimes a problem for those who have just begun to live alone, as well as for those who are newly divorced or widowed.

Start by taking the initiative. Never wait for people to ask you to do something. Instead, ask them first. Among other things, this allows you to befriend people who interest you rather than waiting for a perhaps less interesting person to show an interest in you. If you always wait for others to offer their company, you may find yourself with a much slower and duller social life than you might like. Very recently divorced and widowed people should realize that others may wait for a cue from them that they're ready to socialize; they in particular often have to do something to activate their social lives.

The first step is to find someone to socialize with. Usually this will be someone who's like you—another single, in other words. Obviously you'll also want some married couples to round out your roster of friends, but other singles offer the most immediate, easy access to friendship because they're usually available when you are. You might begin by asking a co-worker, a neighbor, or a friend whether he would like to go to a movie or out to dinner. Never hesitate to be the first one to suggest an activity when you're getting to know someone.

When you invite someone to go somewhere with you, be aware of the other person's budget and related limitations. A divorced mother who's supporting her children may not be able to spend an entire evening out, but she might welcome the chance to meet you for a brief lunch on a day when she's out running errands anyway or to share a cup of coffee or a drink after work.

Always honor plans once you've made them. Your married friends may be casual about loose plans because they won't be hungry for companionship if plans fall through, but singles really count on their social plans. A single might not see anyone else on a Saturday other than the person she's planned to share pizza and a movie with, so once you've made plans, don't cancel except for a very good reason—such as illness or some other emergency.

Being inclusive also helps to expand your social horizons. Obviously you won't want to put together friends who have nothing in common or aren't likely to hit it off with one another, and you don't want always to see your friends in groups. But it's still kinder—and more fun—to include as many people as possible.

To add interest to your life, try to think beyond the usual when getting together with friends. It's easy—almost too easy—to go out to dinner or the movies, but there are a host of other activities that you can do with friends. Try making an exercise date. Plan to do errands with a friend and then treat yourselves to lunch or coffee afterward. Most of us spend far more time than we'd like on errands, and having something to look forward to when they're done is great. Plan some outings—theater parties, hikes, photography expeditions, whatever suits you.

Finally, having urged you to build an active social life, I'm now going to suggest that you not let it get out of hand. Many singles complain that their social lives are either feast or famine, and while this is sometimes tricky to control, it can be done. The most contented people are those who recognize their limits for socializing and stick to them. Those who don't, risk not being very good company.

Similarly, most of us need to discover our limits for being alone and to make sure we have plans when it's time to see people. If you live alone, try to pace your social life so you spend the right amount of time with others—and also get enough time to yourself.

Where to Meet and Mingle

For some, the problem is not turning down invitations, but drumming them up. Many newly single people don't know how to go about meeting people or how to befriend them when they do. The best way to meet people is to follow your interests. Do you love art? Find a lecture series at your local museum or take a guided tour. Do you have a favorite hobby? Search out others who share your interest by joining a club or a group. Are you interested in theater? Join an amateur theater group. Do you relish politics? Volunteer to work on a campaign. Volunteering for anything, in fact, is an excellent way to meet like-minded people.

If you're a newly single parent, join one of several national groups—Parents without Partners is the most well known—made up of people like you. Whatever your interests, there is a club or group organized to promote them.

Don't be afraid to take some risks. You don't have to be a master photographer or an accomplished actress to join a group organized around these activities. Remember, you're trying to make friends, not forge a new career. Besides, however interested everyone is in the group activity, chances are that at least some are there for the same reason you are—to meet new people.

Meeting Potential Dates

The search for new romantic partners isn't all that different from the search for new platonic friends. Start by looking in the same places. It's terrific if you can meet someone whose interests match yours, but if specialized clubs and groups don't turn up anyone interesting, it may be time to join a singles group whose sole purpose is matchmaking. Before you do, though, investigate the group to be sure you'll meet the kinds of people you're looking for.

Another good way to meet people is through friends. Often friends are willing to play matchmaker as soon as you let them know you're ready to date—and sometimes they're ready to play matchmaker even before you're ready. The usual way to put two people together is through a blind date. But if you don't like this idea, ask a friend to invite you and a prospective romantic interest to a party or dinner where you can get acquainted on less formal grounds. And if you don't want anyone to play matchmaker, make this clear as well—politely, of course.

The Etiquette of Singles Mingling

However you choose to meet people, it's important to make the most of the opportunity. For this you need to know how to mingle. Most of us feel a little awkward doing this, so here are some hints to help you succeed:

• Be friendly. Your goal is to meet others, and you may have to wade through a few uninteresting souls to meet a soul mate. Since you can't necessarily tell by looking who's a true soul mate, the best modus operandi is to be extremely gracious to everyone you encounter.

• Be equally kind to everyone. So what if someone is boring you to tears? He or she still might have a cousin or a best friend roaming the room who is just right for you.

• Be interested. Many of us, out of shyness, talk too much about ourselves, especially when meeting new people. We also undoubtedly hope to impress by offering up details of our lives and accomplishments. But a far better way to impress is to show an intense interest in the person you're meeting. This is also in your best interests since it enables you to find out a lot about the person. At singles gatherings it's usually okay to ask questions you might not normally be so quick to ask, such as have they been married or do they have children.

• Be interesting. People like to meet lively, interesting people, so make sure you are one of those active types. Always try to reveal some of your interests when you're talking with someone. Mention that you went skiing last weekend, that you've just joined a photography club, or that you're an avid tennis player.

• Don't lament your plight—whatever it is. Singles who are desperate to get married make a mistake to show their colors like this when they're meeting someone new. (Even your friends won't be so inclined to fix you up if they sense you're feeling desperate.)

However sad you may feel to be divorced or widowed, by the time you're ready to look for a new romantic interest, you should be healed enough not to make your situation the major topic of the evening. It's not necessary to clamp down on your feelings about being never married, or newly divorced, or widowed. For many people these are somber and time-absorbing states, but there is a time and place to discuss them, and that is not when you're out looking for someone to date.

• Finally, personal safety is much more an issue these days than it was even ten or fifteen years ago. Good manners can help you protect yourself. It is acceptable and smart, for example, to lunch with someone before agreeing to dinner, or not to want to invite a new acquaintance into your home right away. The key, though, is to do this graciously. The other person should walk away convinced you're eager to see her again (if you are), not feeling rejected.

One strategy that helps in these situations is to make a preemptive move. Before the other person can suggest coming up to your place for a nightcap, mention that you'd love to ask him up but can't because you have an early morning meeting or some work to do. This lets the other person down gently.

Dating: Who Asks

Women often want to know if they can ask men out on dates, and the answer is an unequivocal yes. But there is a tactful way to do it. Try to arrange to get together for a reason rather than calling for a formal date. For example, let's say you belong to a professional group, at which you've met a very interesting man. A good strategy is to say, "Gee, we seem to be working on very similar projects at work. Maybe we should get together for lunch to talk about this some more." If he's interested, he'll jump at the chance—even if he suspects it's a ploy. If you share a hobby or other interest group, ask him if he would like to get a cup of coffee with you after the meeting.

Remember that when a woman does the asking, she runs the same risk of getting turned down that a man does. And she must also take the hint when someone doesn't want to go out with her. If someone turns you down but says he'll call, then you've pretty much made your move and must wait for the call.

Who Pays for Dates?

This is a big subject in these days of egalitarian social relations. For first dates, the general rule is that whoever asks, pays. Certainly if you invite someone to a concert or other entertainment, you are expected to pay. If your guest has any class, though, he will pick up the tab for something—dinner or a snack—during the evening. The person who extended the invitation may accept or reject this offer.

Most people who date one another regularly eventually work out some means of sharing the expenses. Dating can be an economic burden, and many men and women of all ages feel they must share the tab in one way or another when they date.

When one of you earns far more money than the other, it's all right for the person with more money to pay for most or even all of the social outings. Since men generally earn more than women, this means the man usually ends up picking up the tab—which also corresponds to many people's social values. Some men, and many women, though, can't afford to date if dating means they must pay. In this instance it's up to you to talk about your situation and work out some arrangement that is equitable to both of you. In the early stages, when it is awkward to discuss finances, the best solution may be to plan inexpensive activities. Free concerts, sports activities, hikes, walks, free or inexpensive movies, picnics, and cooking dinner at home are all good possibilities. There is no need to have a specific discussion about your finances unless you want to. You can simply offer a passing conversational reference about your limited resources, and if the other person has any consideration, he will get the message and act accordingly.

Few men above a certain age are willing to let a woman pay for them, so if you're a woman with money in a relationship with a man who has less, you may have to scale down your activities rather than risk hurting your partner. Most men of any age, though, are comfortable letting a woman pick up the tab occasionally.

If you do accept someone's offer to pay for you on a regular basis, good manners dictate that you must still make an occasional effort to balance out the economic disharmony. Once in a while, *you* pick up the tickets for a ball game or concert and treat the other person. Every second or third time you go out for dinner, invite your friend to your place for a good, home-cooked meal.

The Well-Mannered Date

Regardless of who asks and who pays, you'll want to be a well-mannered date. A few guidelines will help make you a skilled dater:

• Be clear about the invitation. When asking someone out, ask for a specific time and activity. Beyond the first or second date, most dates go better when both people have a hand in the planning. It's never polite, though, to ask if someone's free on such-and-such night. This puts the other person on the spot. Most people want to know what they're being invited to do before they accept an invitation.

- Be prompt. If you say you'll pick someone up at eight P.M., then make it a point to arrive exactly at the appointed hour. Similarly, if you've been told to be ready at eight P.M., make sure you are. It's passé to primp for half an hour while your date cools his (or her) heels staring at your cat.

- Be interesting. Yes, it takes some effort to carry on a conversation with a stranger. Yes, dating is, at least initially, an artificial activity. So don't leave everything up to the other person. Scan the newspaper or watch the news and have in mind a couple of subjects you can bring up to get the conversational ball rolling.

- Be interested. Too many people are interested only in putting themselves forward on a date, but you'll really impress your date if you're interested in her. This is one of the rare social occasions when it is acceptable, within limits, to pry into the other person's life. Have at it—and find out whether you really like this person or not.

- Be kind. Even if thirty minutes into the date you have figured out that you're not soul mates, that in fact you're not even destined to have a second date, you are still obligated to be polite. This means you make conversation, you get through the evening, and you deliver the person home at a not unreasonably early hour.

- But don't lead on someone who isn't right for you. We've all had the experience where we've ended what was for us a marvelous evening convinced that we've clicked with our date—yet we never hear from him again. When this happens, someone has overplayed the politeness card, and it's a rude thing to do. Don't say you'll call when you won't, don't make plans you don't intend to carry out, and don't show affection toward someone to whom you feel none.

INTIMACY AND THE NEW SEXUAL ETIQUETTE

An entirely new sexual etiquette has arisen to help us respond to AIDS and other sexually transmitted diseases. Most of us know we need to ask certain questions of any prospective partner, but we aren't sure how to go about it in a polite and nonalienating way. Both men and women today also are concerned with how they can signal a date regarding their sexual intentions. All these feelings, naturally, are magnified when the person dealing with them is newly widowed or divorced.

Sending Signals

Single men and women carry an amazing number of misperceptions regarding each other's intentions that often lead to misleading social behavior. For example, many single men believe all single women are desperate to marry, when in fact many single women, especially those who are economically self-sufficient, are ambivalent about marriage. Single women, in turn, often feel that men have it easy since they are so desirable on the social circuit, when in truth many newly widowed or divorced men are terrified about what is expected of them—and totally unprepared to cope with their new lives.

The best cure for these misperceptions is communication. If someone asks you out, and you're not ready to date yet, then say so, but do it as politely and thoughtfully as you can. Don't turn down the invitation without an explanation. Instead, say, "I really appreciate the invitation, but I'm not ready to go out yet. But it's very kind of you to ask." Once you do accept an invitation, you may still feel the need to establish some limits. This can be done tactfully, perhaps by saying, "I'd love to go to the basketball game with you, but I have to tell you that I can only handle the most casual relationship at this point. I hope you'll understand."

Once this warning has been given, it's up to the other person to decide whether to pursue the relationship. Someone who is looking primarily for a sexual relationship indeed may not see you again. Someone who is willing to keep it casual, usually in the hope that a relationship will develop later, probably will. If someone wants an intimate relationship, physically and emotionally, then you may not hear from him or her again. But at least you have signaled your intentions, and you can then be comfortable when you do go out.

Any single person, in fact, can send advance signals regarding his or her sexual intentions. If you aren't planning a romantic assignation, it is sometimes more tactful to make this clear early in the evening—especially if you believe your date has intentions in this direction. You can comment that you have an early meeting or deadline the next morning or announce that you're tired from the previous day's activities, or, most obviously, you can signal your intention by not inviting your date to your home at the end of the evening.

Most of the time women are the ones who send these signals, but guess what? Often men are quite relieved to receive them. For the man who is not, the signals still mean the same thing. Once a woman has indicated she is not interested in sexual intimacy, the only polite response is to accept her decision—without grumbling, without complaint, and certainly without pressure.

More Serious Sexual Concerns

Many people today are less concerned about telling a prospective sexual partner "no" on any one evening than about the need to check out his or her overall sexual health at the beginning of a relationship. One very savvy woman says she usually brings up the subject by mentioning her own concern about the dangers of sexual relationships these days. If she senses that her partner is on her wavelength, she then suggests that they both be tested for AIDS and other sexually transmitted diseases. (Yes, it has come to this.) Disinterest on a prospective partner's part, she says, is enough to turn her off to the relationship.

Even if they don't insist on an AIDS test, most people today want some kind of information about a partner's past before initiating an intimate relationship. It's acceptable, and even smart, to ask questions about previous partners and other relationships. If your date assumes your questions are prompted by jealousy, explain that you simply want to know more about him or her.

Your date will probably realize that you're actually trying to start a conversation about each other's sexual health. While it used to be gauche to ask or talk about past loves, these days it's not only accepted but expected. It's still polite, though, to skip the lurid details. That's *not* what your date is fishing for when he makes inquiries about your past life. And of course, turnabout is fair play. If you ask questions, you must expect to answer some yourself.

Today it is imperative that sexually active couples use condoms, and typically it is the woman who brings up this sometimes touchy subject. Some women carry them so their partners can't beg off by saying they don't have one. A friend says that when a relationship has reached a certain stage of intimacy, she playfully brings up the fact that she and her partner might be spending the night together sometime soon. In the same light tone, she also makes it clear that she expects that a condom will be used. She said most men don't object to waiting another few days—and so far, all her dates have shown up prepared.

Presents for Lovers

Many otherwise sophisticated people become nervous when it's time to give a gift to someone they're romantically involved with. I suspect that, consciously or subconsciously, we want to use gifts to deepen a relationship or to read a deeper involvement into the relationship than is actually there. Whatever the reason, many a relationship has been ruined by too much intimacy too soon in this area. Remember, you can always buy each other intimate and expensive presents after you're in a committed relationship, but it's very hard to undo the damage that a too intimate gift wreaks on a relationship when given prematurely.

The first rule of giving gifts to relatively new lovers, is to keep them low key—especially if you're not sure you're both equally committed to the relationship. Generally this means not giving gifts that are either too expensive or too intimate. In the too expensive category are real jewelry (including watches), electronic equipment, and furs. A gift is too intimate if it gives the impression that one person is supporting another. Basic clothes, such as a coat, would be inappropriate, while luxury items, such as a cashmere sweater, would not be. Intimate undergarments, needless to say, are unacceptable early on in a relationship.

While a gift shouldn't be too intimate, it should be personal. A friend was once crushed when a man she had been dating for several months gave her a very impersonal datebook for Christmas—the kind of gift one sends to a business associate. The gift sent a definite message, and indeed the relationship ended days later.

Good personal but not overly intimate presents include

compact discs, books, small leather items (a really nice datebook is okay!), desk accessories (but not a photograph of you—not yet, anyway), and small gadgets. Among clothing items, you might give a scarf or a nice sweater, but not socks, underwear, or pajamas.

LIVING TOGETHER

Socially, cohabiting couples are treated like married couples. They are invited to family gatherings, weddings, and other events just as a married couple would be. For most couples, problems arise only when they're in a new environment, such as a new job, and haven't yet declared their unmarried status.

At such times it's best to maneuver tactfully. When it's time for the annual office party, exercise discretion, based on what you perceive to be your employer's view of your situation. If you're allowed to bring a guest, then there's no problem. You bring your significant other and introduce him by his name. No further comment is called for, no matter how much others may pry—unless, of course, you're willing to give up information.

If you're not invited to bring a guest, then it will be up to you how much you want to push the situation—and reveal about your private life. This may be the time to tell your boss that you live with someone and would like to bring her. But don't forget that however important your relationship is, your career matters as well. For example, if you know your living arrangements will be frowned upon, it might be better to bite the bullet and not insist on bringing your lover to the office party.

A big question for couples who live together is how to introduce each other. Since it isn't necessary to disclose your personal relationship to others, you can say, "I'd like you to meet Ted Jones," and leave it at that. If you want to, you can add, "We live together," but you are never under any obligation to do so.

Cohabiting (or other longtime) couples often face another hurdle: what happens when they visit their parents. Should cohabiting couples expect to share a room when they visit their parents, and if so, who brings up the subject? The answer will not please everyone. But in fact it is up to the host or hostess—even when they are your parents—to decide what the sleeping arrangements will be. If they do not object to your sharing a room, they will put you in one together. If they do, you will almost certainly be given separate sleeping quarters. If this doesn't suit you, your option is not to protest or argue, but to get a motel room or stay with other friends or relatives. Since feelings are rarely changed on this delicate subject, most cohabiting couples and their families agree not to try to persuade the other side to their point of view.

SAME-SEX RELATIONSHIPS

However unaccepting the world can be of straight lovers' lives, it is unfortunately even less accepting of same-sex relationships. Yet I am often asked questions by straight people who are eager to include their gay and lesbian friends in activities and events—and unsure how best to go about doing this. Same-sex couples should be treated like any other married or cohabiting couple. This means that one partner should not be invited to a social gathering without including the other one.

As for introductions, the same advice that applies to heterosexual couples applies here. Introduce your partner by saying, "This is Mary Smith." There is never any need to explain more, unless you want to. Curious people should take note: It is neither polite nor pertinent to inquire about—or hint at—another person's sexual orientation, practices, or living arrangements.

GETTING THROUGH THE HOLIDAYS

For many singles the holidays are a depressing time, something merely to be "gotten through." Here are some ideas that may help make them easier to deal with socially:

• Decide what you want to do—and then do it politely. If it's too depressing to be with your family, then spend the holidays with friends. But whoever you are avoiding, try to do so graciously. Let people know you're grateful to be invited somewhere, and tell them how sorry you are to have made other plans. If you must attend a gathering, go for a brief time, even if you have to tell a white lie about the need to go somewhere else.

• Don't plan too much. Be firm but polite about rejecting the invitations that will put you into overdrive—or simply won't cheer you up.

• Don't avoid married couples' social gatherings. Savvy hosts and hostesses always mix attached and unattached people, and there's nothing wrong with taking advantage of the mix—even if the occasion *is* New Year's Eve. It does take a little nerve to go out alone, but those of us who have overcome this obstacle have learned that it's possible to have a very good time.

• Treat yourself to a special social occasion. A friend of mine always balances out her family obligations, which aren't very pleasant for her, with a special tea she gives for her closest friends. It's a festive occasion that everyone looks forward to.

• Do something kind for someone else. A great way to

shake the holiday blues is to do something for someone who is less well off. Etiquette is about far more than following a set of rules—it's about how you live your life socially. And there are few things more rewarding than extending a helping hand to someone who needs it. So volunteer to deliver holiday meals to shut-ins or the elderly. Go to the post office and pick up a letter a child has written to Santa, and then give that child Christmas. Plan to prepare or serve meals at a soup kitchen. I guarantee it'll lift your spirits. You'll feel wonderful, and who knows—you may meet like-minded singles!

LIFE AFTER A DIVORCE OR A DEATH

One of the hardest things any of us ever has to do is begin a new social life after losing a partner to death or divorce. Sooner or later, though, most people do want to resume one and may even want to cast about for a new partner.

You know in your heart when you're emotionally ready to date again, but you may not be sure when it is socially acceptable to do so. The answer is that it is acceptable to resume your social life—in every aspect—whenever you feel comfortable with it. We do not demand formal mourning of anyone these days. After a partner has died, most people resume their normal activities within a week or two, and many feel ready to date again within six months to a year. For others, several years are required. What's important is not to push in either direction.

When you're separated, there may be a legal impediment to resuming a social life, which is that you're still married. The days are gone when a separated person could not date, and this is probably good, given how drawn out divorces tend to be. But a few things remain in bad taste.

One is to date indiscreetly when you have just separated.

If the divorce is held up and takes months or even years to complete, then you obviously will start dating again. But to date immediately after a separation sends a signal that you may prefer not to send about why your marriage ended. And if you are involved with someone when you separate, it's still better—socially speaking—to keep the relationship under wraps for at least a few months.

Another behavior lacking in good taste is to announce plans to marry while you are still married to someone else. Only slightly less tacky, no matter how drawn out your divorce has been, is to marry within weeks of ending a marriage. At minimum, unless there is a very good reason, it's better to wait at least two or three months, especially if children are involved.

Taking off Wedding Rings

Divorced people usually have little trouble figuring out when it's time to remove a wedding ring, but widows and widowers are less sure about when and whether they should remove their rings. One thing is certain: If you hope to remarry, it's best to remove your wedding band. But it's understandable that you may not feel like doing this for several months or even years.

Many widows continue to wear their engagement ring, although they usually switch it to the right hand. If your new partner objects to your wearing the engagement ring given to you by your previous husband, then it's time either to pass it on to a daughter or daughter-in-law or to have it reset into another piece of jewelry.

Photos and Mementos

Photographs and other mementos of a loved one can pose another problem. After losing a partner to death, you'll find it comforting to have these things around. And if you have children, you may want to keep photos of your ex-husband as well.

Once you start a social life, though, their presence may cause anyone you date to wonder if you are ready to commit yourself again. I advise a middle-of-the-road approach: Take down the wall of photos of your late husband (and perhaps distribute them to your children), but allow yourself one or two photos if you need to, displayed in a discreet, out-of-the-way place. If you can't bear to do even this, it may say something about your readiness to date, and you may need to wait a while longer.

Conversation about Your Former Partner

In our society we tend to put away the dead quickly—and perhaps dwell too much on our ex-spouses. You should be comfortable talking about your deceased partner, but you also need to realize that this will be a delicate subject once you start to date again. Too much conversation about your loss, like too many photos in your living room, sends a message that perhaps you aren't ready to date yet. And anyone you date may well read this as a message to move on.

On the other hand, part of getting acquainted with a new romantic interest involves sharing your past life—and that means talking about your partner. It doesn't matter who brings up the subject, but when it does come up, explain a little bit—what your partner did, what your relationship was like—and then ask your date whether he or she is comfortable discussing this. A secure person won't mind and will even welcome the opportunity to learn more about you, but he or she also won't want to dwell on your past relationships. It's important to keep this in mind when you're trying to forge a new relationship.

Your Name after a Death or a Divorce

A woman's name doesn't change after she is widowed. She continues to be Mrs. John Anderson. Many women today, however, choose to use their first names and their husband's last names anyway, as in Mrs. Mary Anderson. This used to connote a divorced woman, but today it is just as often the name of a married or a widowed woman.

Many women don't have to worry about what name to use after a divorce because they didn't change their names when they married. A divorced woman who has been Mrs. John Anderson, however, doesn't continue to use this name after her divorce. Among other things, it will cause awkward mixups if there is a second Mrs. John Anderson. After her divorce, Mrs. John Anderson at her own discretion becomes Mrs. (or Ms.) Mary Anderson or, more formally, Mrs. Willetts Anderson, a combination of her maiden and married name. Many women also revert to their maiden names.

A FEW YEARS AGO, AN ETIQUETTE BOOK WOULD NEVER have included a chapter on single life. To be single was to be odd, out of step with a mostly married world. These days, though, more than half of the adult population for one reason or another—late marriage, divorce, death—spends a sizable chunk of time living the single life. There is much to be made of these periods in our lives. They give us not only an opportunity to know ourselves better, but also a chance to expand our social horizons in truly interesting ways. One of the best things we can do for ourselves is to take full advantage of the social opportunities that being single offer.

Chapter 3

FRIENDSHIPS

FRIENDS ARE ONE OF THE GREAT TREASURES OF LIFE, YET all too often we fail to cultivate and nurture them. In this chapter we'll talk about how you can graciously maintain these special treasures.

GREETING FRIENDS

Friends greet one another informally in the United States. Europeans shake hands or kiss every time they greet, and many Asians bow, but Americans simply say hello. We may shake hands after a long absence or even throw an arm around a friend on occasion, but this is not our regular form of greeting.

Shaking Hands

When we do shake hands, Americans in particular favor a strong handshake—and indeed often (erroneously) assume this is a sign of a strong character. Regardless of how you view handshaking, it's important to know how to do it—and a surprising number of people don't seem to have gotten the hang of this.

Not too long ago, the rules about handshaking were considerably more rigid than they are today. A man never extended his hand first to a lady, for example. Not only did a gentleman wait for a lady to offer her hand, but when she did, you could be sure that a white glove—then part of every lady's outfit—prevented any real pressing of the flesh. In another equally archaic gesture, a man was expected to remove his glove even on the coldest days to shake hands with a woman, while a woman never removed hers.

Today, fortunately, we live more egalitarian lives. A man no longer need quake in fear that a woman will not consider him socially acceptable enough to shake hands with. And women, if they are wearing gloves at all, often find themselves apologizing for them and even pulling them off before they shake hands. The mere act of handshaking is no longer an awe-inspiring occasion, but there are still a few rules to follow:

• Extend a firm hand. Never offer a limp one. If you are not sure whether your handshake is firm enough, shake with a friend and ask for an honest opinion. Then remedy the situation, if necessary.

• Keep the handshake fairly brief. Note the key word here is "fairly." We Americans don't do the two quick pumps of the French, but neither do most people appreciate being caught in someone's grasp for longer than, say, four or five pumps. Only queens and very old ladies are allowed to hang on when they shake hands—and queens rarely avail themselves of this opportunity.

• Do stand when you are planning to shake hands with someone—or even when greeting a friend whom you do not ordinarily shake hands with. The only exceptions are the ill, the frail, nursing mothers, and those physically unable to stand. Women used not to stand to meet others, but today the gracious woman does whenever possible.

• The rule on gloves is now based on practicality, perhaps because gloves today are worn only for practical reasons, such as the weather. If it is chilly, people of either sex may keep on their gloves to shake hands. For formal or ceremonial occasions when a woman may be wearing gloves purely as a fashion statement, she can keep them on when shaking hands, whereas a man in the same situation should remove his.

Kissing

Except for a few parts of America such as Los Angeles and New York City, Americans do not kiss friends hello and good-bye. And, in fact, in many parts of the country, people would be uncomfortable doing this.

If kissing does not suit you, and you find yourself in a kissing crowd, then it is up to you to let people know—tactfully, of course—that this is not your favorite form of greeting. You can say something like this: "I know everyone in our crowd likes to kiss, but I guess I'm just not the kissing type." Most people will take the hint.

If you are a kisser, try to sense when someone does not particularly enjoy this form of greeting and refrain. Remember too that kissing, even when done as a formal greeting, should always be spontaneous. Never ask someone to kiss you or assume they want to. Finally, do not kiss when you are ill—or getting ill. No one appreciates being handed a cold or, worse, the flu. So if you are ailing, or even if you suspect you are on the verge of illness, the only polite thing to do is beg off.

When to Greet Friends

People have become remarkably casual about greeting friends. I am always a little shocked to enter someone's house and find that the hostess barely greets me—not, I have begun to suspect, because she's sorry she invited me, but because in general she does not know how to welcome her guests. This is perhaps an unfortunate result of years of casual living. There are certain times when you should "formally" greet a friend, even someone you have seen just a few hours earlier. For example, when someone comes to your home, you should stand up, go to the door, and say hello. And when someone leaves your home it's the same routine: Stand up, walk them to the door, and say good-bye.

As a guest, you have some obligations as well. Whenever you arrive at someone's home, your first gesture should be to go up to the host and hostess to say hello. The same thing applies when you are leaving. Even at a large party, always make your way over to the host and/or hostess to say good night—and also, of course, to thank them for a wonderful time.

Greetings on the Street

There are a few occasions when greetings are kept brief, and no one should be offended by this. These include early morning encounters or greetings to neighbors you pass repeatedly in the course of a day. It would be silly to expect to engage in a conversation with everyone you see every time you see them. In such instances it is perfectly appropriate and not the least bit unfriendly simply to nod as you pass one another.

INTRODUCTIONS

Many people feel shy about making introductions, but there is no reason for this. Graceful introductions are something we should all strive for—and fortunately they are easy to master. The following three guidelines will enable you to make all introductions easily and graciously:

- Introduce men to women, as in "Leona, I'd like to introduce George Samuels."
- Introduce younger people to older people, as in "Grandmother, I'd like you to meet my school friend Shelley Martin."
- Introduce less important people to more important people, as in "Mr. President, may I present my sister, Rose O'Grady?"

Or "Mayor James, I'd like you to meet my mother, Edith Still."

Or: "Reverend Riley, I'd like to present my husband, Tim Sawyer."

As a rule, you do not have to decide who the "important" people are. They are those who hold public or other significant semipublic positions, clergypeople, and other dignitaries. Informally you can say, "I'd like you to meet . . ." or, "Let me introduce . . ." More formally, such as when a dignitary is involved, you might choose to say, "I'd like to present . . ."

What to Say When You Are Introduced

The appropriate response upon meeting someone is, "I am pleased to meet you," "How do you do," or, simplest of all, "Hello." Most of the time you should resist the urge to go on about how much you have heard about the person you are meeting; more often than not this produces discomfort rather than pleasure. If you are meeting a good friend of a friend, however, and you feel quite friendly toward the person, then it may be appropriate to add a few complimentary phrases.

Meeting the Physically Infirm

Many people are unsure what to do when meeting someone who is obviously physically infirm and may not be able to shake hands. In this situation it is best to let that person take the lead. Some will extend the left hand instead of the right one or an arm instead of a hand, while others prefer not to shake hands. Since some physically impaired people may prefer not to be touched at all, always wait for a cue from the other person if there is any question.

Meeting the Elderly

It is also a good idea to let the elderly of any sex initiate handshaking or any other kind of physical greeting, since they too may not feel strong enough or be physically able to handle bear hugs or even a handshake.

The Polite Bow

Whether or not you shake hands with someone you meet, it is always appropriate to give a slight bow of acknowledgment. To do this, bend from the waist very slightly. Children, on the other hand, are almost never taught to curtsey or bow in any formal way these days.

What to Call the Person You Just Met

We are definitely a first-name society, but a bit of discretion upon first meetings, especially those with public officials, dignitaries, and elderly people, goes a long way.

Sometimes the person making the introduction offers a valuable clue. It is helpful, for instance, if a friend says, "I'd like you to meet my good friend and teacher, Dr. Robert Walsh, whom everyone calls Bob." But if you are introduced to "Reverend William Smiley," you can probably surmise that he prefers "Reverend Smiley" to "Bill."

Similarly, if a friend introduces a parent as "Mrs. Smith," consider it a pretty broad hint that Mrs. Smith prefers to be called Mrs. Smith. Even if you are introduced to Mary Smith, it is gracious to err on the side of formality until invited to do otherwise. Remember, someone can always ask you to call him by his first name, but there is virtually no polite way to explain that a little more formality would have been preferred.

HOW TO MAKE SPARKLING CONVERSATION

For many of us, it is not being introduced to someone but what we do afterward that proves difficult. Quite a few people are shy about talking to others they do not know well.

And it is no wonder. There is an art to conversation and even more of one to making small talk. Fortunately it is something that is easily mastered. Here are a few hints on making fascinating conversation with virtually anyone—the person you just met as well as the complete stranger sitting next to you at a dinner party.

• You go first. Almost everyone feels at least some awkwardness about meeting strangers and is inevitably grateful for any conversational gambit that comes her way. Therefore you be the one to start the conversation.

• Prepare yourself in advance for conversation. Use radio, television, articles, and books you have read as fodder for conversation. This may sound calculated, but I am shy enough that even after years of talking to strangers, I still prepare in a rather obvious way before spending an evening in company. When I am going out for the evening, I make a point of watching the news or reading the newspaper more thoroughly than usual just so I'll have a few current topics to bring up.

• Look for a shared or common interest. The simplest way into any conversation is to find out what you have in common—which may be only the person who brought you together. Ask your conversation partner how he knows either the person who introduced you or the host.

• Ask questions that are not dead end, especially ones that require some thought. *How, why,* and *what* are the magic words here. "I see you're carrying a mystery by Jane Scarey. What do you like about her writing?" Or, more generally: "What is it, do you think, that has made her so enormously popular?" Note the difference between this and saying, "Do you like her writing?" When put to a shy person, such a dead-end question will bring the conversation to a complete stop.

- Topical questions, provided they are not too political, make for good conversation. "What did you think about the president's press conference?"
- Politely personal questions can be wonderful openers. Everyone likes to talk about himself or herself. One of the best entrees into conversation is to follow up personal information with an interesting question, such as "How did you happen to live in India for five years?" Or you might say: "You're using a parasol. What a great idea in this sunshine." Or, "I see you are carrying a backpack. Do you find that more convenient than a purse?"
- Avoid controversial or unsuitable subjects. Some subjects of conversation are still taboo. This means avoiding politics, religion, illness, and our domestic lives. Although the last entry on this list may surprise you, the fact is that very few people are fascinated with stories about your children, your domestic difficulties (or raging successes, for that matter), or how you house-broke your pet.
- Don't gossip. It's tantalizing, I know, but it is never kind to put yourself at ease at the expense of another person. Besides, you never know whom you are talking to. A friend once confessed to me her horror when she made a disparaging comment about a man at a garden party only to have the woman to whom she'd made the comment turn to her and say, "That's my brother."
- Smile. We often do not fully appreciate how much body language communicates. If you do not believe this, just survey a room of strangers to see whom you would most like to approach. Is it the person with the scowl lurking in a corner or the smiling person who is already happily engaged in a conversation with several others?
- Learn to be a good listener. Why not? This is the easy part of conversation. Look at the person in a friendly way. Do not fidget with the flatware, cast your eyes around the

room, or stare off into the distance. Really pay attention. Many a famous conversationalist is really a famous listener, and it's so easy.

• Don't repeat. Don't ramble. When you do get a chance to talk, don't drive away the other person. Keep your half of the conversation relatively short and to the point.

• Don't preach. It's wonderful that you just stopped smoking or lost twenty pounds, but it doesn't give you the right to proselytize to others who have not yet managed these feats—and it does nothing to make you a lively conversationalist. If anything, you will push people away.

• Finally, if all else fails, bring up the weather, but try not to ask a dead-end question about it. Try to ask a what, why, or how question that encourages the other person to really talk to you.

When You Are Stuck with a Conversational Dud

If given any encouragement, most people will manage to hold up their end of a conversation, and they are usually grateful to you for giving them a chance to do so. But all of us have also been stuck with a real dud—someone who cannot or will not respond, a stuffed shirt, a nonstop talker, or worse, a true bore.

When this happens, you are allowed to take defensive action and get away, unless of course you are seated next to the person at dinner (and even then you can always talk more to the person on the other side of you). It is important to give the other person a chance, but once you have determined that your partner cannot be drawn out or talked with in a comfortable manner, you may feel free to turn your attention elsewhere.

The easiest way to get away from a bore (or boor) is simply to excuse yourself, on the pretense of greeting a friend, getting another drink, getting food, or going to the bathroom. When you begin to recirculate, it is acceptable to head in another direction. Another ploy is to move yourself and the bore into a larger group, which will then absorb him and leave you free to go on your merry way. Finally, you can introduce the person to someone else and hope that he is that person's cup of tea.

Become a Large-Talk Savant

We all worry about small talk, but for some people the real problem arises when a friend wants to engage in a serious conversation, usually about something that is troubling him or her in a highly personal way.

When a friend comes to you with a big problem, listen sympathetically. Don't jump in with suggestions until your friend has finished the story—and even then, do not be so sure that suggestions and advice are actually being solicited. Most people at such times need a sympathetic ear—and no more. Beyond that there may be little you can or need to do except reassure your friend that you are there for her, that you will respect whatever decision she makes, and that you are always available to listen. Such conversations are usually in confidence, even if this is not specifically discussed. A friend does not share another friend's most intimate secrets with anyone.

Flattery

Flattery can be a wonderful social lubricant. But it must be used correctly. All of us recognize when we are being given insincere or manipulative compliments, and virtually no one enjoys them.

Therefore, the first rule of flattery is to make sure it is

sincere. We have all known someone who oozes compliments—to the point where we no longer believe even the teeniest one. Apart from this, a specific compliment is always better than a nonspecific one. For example, given a chance to tell a friend he looks good or that his tie is very witty, always opt for the latter.

Be careful about complimenting strangers or brand-new acquaintances. It presumes an acquaintanceship that does not exist. This isn't to say that you can't loft the occasional general compliment to get a conversation going, but you should never use flattery to ingratiate yourself with others. It always sounds false.

Humor

Humor, too, should be used sparingly in public and in general conversation. This is not to say that you cannot tell the occasional funny story or anecdote, merely that you should not overdo it. There are always people whose entire conversation consists of one funny (or, more often, not so funny) story after another. When used defensively this way, humor becomes a shield, making it impossible for anyone to get to know you.

Even more important, never use humor to deride or poke fun at someone or something else. Jokes that are aimed at one group or at religious, political, or social values are never appropriate and are always offensive.

Coping with Prejudice

Not very far removed from a bad joke is prejudice, which is inappropriate under any circumstances. Prejudice exists only to make some people feel like outsiders and to make others, particularly the person exhibiting the prejudice, feel like insiders. This is the very antithesis of what good manners are all about.

The issue for most people, though, is what to do when someone tells a joke or makes a disparaging comment about another person or group. Do you laugh even though you do not think the comment is funny? Do you snarl and thus find yourself being rude to someone? Most of us try for something in between, especially when we—and the offender— are someone's guest. But this is one social occasion when it is perfectly appropriate to let another person know that you find his behavior or conversation distasteful.

There are several ways short of causing a public scene to do this. At the most benign, you can simply not respond. Don't nod in agreement, don't laugh at the joke, don't pretend to go along.

Unfortunately, most prejudiced people are blind to the fact that the entire world does not agree with them. This is why it is also perfectly acceptable, and sometimes even incumbent upon you, to say, "I'm sorry, but I don't agree with you," or, "You'll understand if I don't find that very funny." If the person continues (which often happens once you react with annoyance), excuse yourself and walk away.

Questions You Should Not Ask

Whether among friends or acquaintances, some subjects are off limits. These may vary slightly from person to person, or even from friendship to friendship, but in general, for example, personal finances are not open to discussion. People have a right to privacy about what they earn and how much they paid for something. Most of us also do not want to discuss the details of our romantic or domestic lives with anyone except intimate friends.

A surprising number of people are unwilling to disclose

their age. It is in midlife that many lose interest in announcing their age. But by the time a senior citizen makes it to
ripe old age, he or she is usually delighted to tell you—
sometimes repeatedly—how old he or she is.

Other off-limit topics are illnesses and personal troubles. I
have a friend whose daughter was ill for many years. For a
long time there was no diagnosis. Doctors simply could not
figure out what was wrong with her. During this time, my
friend was often deeply troubled about her child, but she
repeatedly declined to discuss it.

Initially I felt left out, but I soon came to realize this was
her way of dealing with what felt at the time like an overwhelming problem. I saw that the only polite—and kind—
response was to stop asking for details. I continued to ask
about her daughter in the most general way and expressed
my sympathy when it seemed appropriate to do so. But I
stopped asking any direct questions.

Several years later she confirmed my analysis of her feelings when she mentioned how much she had appreciated
the "quiet show of support." She said she simply could not
bear to discuss the problem at the time. Good and supportive friends do not press friends to discuss topics they do not
wish to talk about.

Questions You Would Rather Not Answer

When you are the put-upon person who is being asked a too
personal question, it is sometimes difficult to know how to
respond politely. Many at first pretend they have not heard
the troublesome question and then try to change the subject—quickly. But avoidance, except perhaps with a repeat
offender, has a rude edge. An interesting alternative ap-
peared years ago in an Ann Landers column, and it has
proved surprisingly effective. When asked an inappropriate

question, you can laughingly ask, "Why in the world would you want to know that?" All but the most intrepid snoopers usually take this hint—if only because it holds a mirror up to their motives.

Alternately, you can give a totally ridiculous answer. When a friend's sister asked how much her husband had spent on a piece of jewelry he had given her, my friend laughed and said, "Oh, I hope millions and millions of dollars." Other people prefer a more direct response, although these sometimes risk sounding condescending. But when someone is really nosy, nothing may work except telling the person point-blank, "I am sorry, but I am really not comfortable discussing that subject."

THE ART OF MAINTAINING A FRIEND

All friendships need maintenance. Friends need to spend time together, time when they can enjoy the common interests that brought them together in the first place.

It does not matter who calls whom to make plans as long as you both do your share over time. We have all suffered through friends who cannot be bothered to pick up the phone but then profess undying friendship when we call them. Yet to keep a friendship on an even keel, both parties need to do their part, not every day or every week, but certainly over the long run. Still, if you have not seen a friend for a while, even if you initiated your last get-together, there is no reason not to initiate another one—as long as the friendship is not entirely out of balance.

In between visits, there are other things you can do to keep a friendship alive. Many friends maintain a relationship via the telephone; another good way is to drop the occasional note—especially one in which you enclose a clipping from a magazine or newspaper that has some meaning.

One issue that sometimes arises between friends, especially in the early stages, is who pays when you go out. Most friends share expenses these days, regardless of age and sex. Years ago men and women rarely maintained platonic friendships, so this question did not come up; but today, when men and women are often truly "just friends," the bill is split down the middle just as it would be with same-sex friends.

A slightly different problem arises when one friend can afford to go to more expensive places than the other. We should always strive to be sensitive to what our friends can spend, but sometimes it is not so easy to know this. In these cases it is up to the person who cannot afford the fancy restaurant to make this clear. There is no reason to sound martyred or embarrassed over restricted circumstances or even to offer much of an excuse. When plans are being made, simply say, "I'd prefer to go somewhere else," or even, "That's a bit pricey for me right now. Can we settle on another place?" Once someone has said this, it is up to others to graciously accommodate such a request without further comment.

Gifts among Friends

Friends often exchange gifts. Typical occasions include holidays and birthdays, but I have one friend who would not dream of giving me a present on these occasions but always pops up with something unusual when I least expect it. Often she buys her presents when she travels.

In choosing a gift for a friend, try to find something that appeals to your friend's interests and tastes—and not simply your own. Keep in mind that small gifts are just as wonderful as large gifts (sometimes more so!). Gift giving among friends should never become competitive.

If you cannot afford to give gifts, then you can avoid the gift exchange. Even those of us who can afford some gifts cannot afford an ever-expanding gift list. It is generally easier not to start exchanging gifts than to stop, which is why many people tell friends in advance of gift-giving occasions that they would prefer not to exchange gifts. This should always be said with great tact. For example, you might say, "I'd love to exchange presents with you at Christmas, but I have so many family obligations that I'm afraid I can't." We should never avoid honesty in this situation, especially because more often than not, the other person is relieved not to have another name to add to his guest list.

Alternately, if your means are limited, you can give a friend a small gift. Any real friend will take the hint and do the same in return. But if a friend persists in giving expensive gifts, then you are free to accept them and continue to give within your means.

Hostess Gifts

Hostess or host gifts are given when we attend a dinner party or stay overnight at someone's home. They need not be given to family members and friends with whom you have a regular, informal exchange, but on more formal occasions these small gifts are de rigueur.

Hostess gifts are usually not personal; rather, they are something for the house. Instead of the ubiquitous bouquet or bottle of wine, consider taking a jar of gourmet mustard or vinegar, a pound of really good coffee or tea, or a small kitchen appliance. Such interesting gifts are often a welcome change of pace.

FRIENDS HELPING FRIENDS

Recently I watched a frail elderly friend lift her groceries one by one from the grocery cart to the counter. When she bent over to retrieve a melon, I could stand it no longer. Without asking whether she needed—or wanted—my help, I plunged in, picked up the melon, and set it victoriously on the counter. To her credit, she looked me straight in the eye when she said, "I understand that your intention was to help, but I would rather do that myself."

When I got done soothing my ruffled feathers and vowing never again to help out a friend, I began to understand what she was saying—she had not asked for help, and she had every right not to want it. The lesson is simple: Before we offer to help friends, we should consider whether our assistance in any way impinges on their independence, creates a debt that cannot be repaid, or hurts rather than helps. Help, when offered, should always be tactfully and even subtly given, and it should never be forced on anyone. A helping hand often carries a burden, and people who cannot reciprocate feel uncomfortable accepting others' help. Someone may want to do something without assistance, as in my friend's case, such as getting a little exercise by hefting a melon.

There are times, though, when help is appreciated and readily accepted. We should always offer to give a hand with packages, open doors, lend food when a friend is out of something, or otherwise help with projects. Sometimes it is the smallest degree of assistance that is most appreciated.

Letting Friends Reciprocate

When we do help a friend, we should always let that person reciprocate. A friend of mine takes her elderly aunt to a nice hotel for tea (something the aunt cannot afford on her pensioner's income) four or five times a year. In return, the aunt insists on watering her niece's plants when she is out of town. It is a small favor, and one the niece would gladly find someone else to do, but she knows this is her aunt's way of paying her back—so she does not deny her this opportunity.

When a Friend's Help Is Overweening

Sometimes friends insist on helping in inappropriate ways. For example, someone who insists on picking up the tab every time we eat out may think he is doing everyone a big favor; in fact, his behavior may give offense, to say nothing of putting others in a difficult spot. How can we possibly ask this person to dine with us as often as we might like? We do such friends a favor when we gently let them know that they are putting us on the spot. And in such instances the friendly but direct approach often works best. Offer your friend your broadest smile as you say, "It's so nice of you to pick up the tab each time, but I worry that I won't feel so comfortable calling you whenever I feel like it."

Assistance should be given in subtle and tactful ways. One friend who was suffering a financial setback confided to me that she had been forced to cut flowers out of her life because of budget restrictions. My impulse was to show up on her doorstep once a week with them, but I resisted the urge. This did not, however, stop me from taking flowers to her every once in a while, a gesture that I hoped was more subtle than my first urge.

Helping an Ill Friend

Another time help is needed is when someone is ill. When illness strikes, people usually need to count on their friends for a few extra favors—from entertainment of a bedridden patient to picking up groceries or dry cleaning. You can even suggest what you might be able to do.

As soon as you learn a friend is ill, call his house and ask what you can do to help. Don't insist on speaking to your friend, though, as he may not feel up to talking on the telephone. If visits are encouraged, then by all means pay a call. And if they are discouraged, find other ways to stay in touch. Send cards and notes to cheer up your friend. Small gifts are welcome as well.

Gifts for Sick Friends

Some presents are appropriate for ill friends and some are not. For example, it is often better not to send highly scented flowers to a sickroom, and some hospitals no longer permit cut flowers of any kind because of the bacteria that can grow in the water. Plants are generally welcome, even flowering ones, provided they are not highly scented.

But ill people get lots of flowers and plants, and if you really want to be creative, look for other kinds of gifts. One favorite of mine is soap. I try to find it in unusual and silly shapes. A back brush or a good hairbrush makes a nice gift, as does a good (but again not overly scented) body lotion. Send or take a sick friend a stack of magazines or a new book. A video or, better yet, a package of several favorite movies is often appreciated.

Visiting Sick Friends

When you do plan to pay a visit to a sick friend, be sure to call first. And make it clear that you will understand a last-minute cancellation. People's moods can change swiftly when they are sick, and friends should be accepting of this. Keep visits short. Even though they may protest, ill people need rest to recuperate; and often when people don't feel well, they don't know how to say that they need to rest. Visit for a short period, and make it clear that you will be back again soon—a cheerful prospect to someone who is laid up in bed. The exception, of course, is when you are spelling a caretaker. Then you should ask in advance how long you will be needed and make sure you are available the whole time.

Finally, if a friend is ill for a long time, keep visiting, keep calling, and keep writing brief notes. The initial flurry of attention often wanes during a long illness, and that's when people really appreciate the friends who continue to call or visit.

WHEN IT IS TIME TO END A FRIENDSHIP

Occasionally you may need to end a friendship. The realization that you no longer care to be friends with someone is never a particularly comfortable one, but there are times when such a decision is appropriate.

Friends can grow apart, usually because their interests or their lives have changed so much that they no longer have enough in common to maintain the friendship. At these times most friendships die a natural death. One or both of you will stop calling the other, and the friendship simply dwindles out. There are no hard feelings, and no explanations may be necessary.

But sometimes a friendship suffers a rupture. A friend does something we cannot forgive, and we do not wish to continue the relationship. It may not be possible to end a ruptured friendship graciously. But if the person wants to know why, you should certainly explain the reason you no longer intend to be friends. The reverse is also true, of course. If someone shows no interest in why you are no longer friends, then don't force the issue. Simply let the friendship die out.

Sadly, we also lose friends because we do not take the time or make the effort to maintain the friendship, even though we would like to. This is an era in which people take a perverse pride in being busy—too busy even to maintain friendships. We profess a need to spend more time together and then do little or nothing about it. Yet this is something we can change if we want to.

FRIENDSHIP IS ONE OF OUR MOST VALUABLE RESOURCES. IT flourishes best, like a garden, when it is cultivated at least a little bit—but not too much. It behooves all of us to take stock of the state of our friendships on occasion. We should decide how much they matter and then do something to maintain them—some small act of kindness such as sending a note or small present, going out of the way to pay a visit, or arranging a special treat.

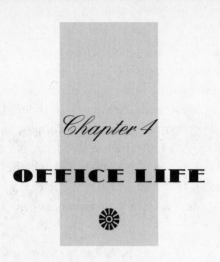

Chapter 4

OFFICE LIFE

MOST BOSSES EXPECT THEIR EMPLOYEES TO GET ALONG with one another and, more important, to get along with clients and customers. This means that however important your job skills are, they may not count for much if you don't also have some people skills. Fortunately, getting along with people usually boils down to simple, everyday courtesy.

REPRESENTING YOUR EMPLOYER

When you work for a company, you are its representative to the outside world. For this reason, everyone from a secretary to a CEO should know how to greet visitors and make them feel comfortable.

Both men and women should stand to greet visitors who come into their office. Co-workers also should be given a warm greeting, but you need not rise each time one comes into your office. For a visitor, though, your hand should be extended just as it would be if you were the host in your own home. Ask the person to sit down; and if there is a choice of seats, you may want to wave him into one.

Many managers and executives sit behind their desks when talking to co-workers and customers, but it is more gracious to move a conversation out to a sofa or two occasional chairs. Visitors should be asked whether they would like a beverage. If the answer is yes, the manager should get the drink or ask a secretary or assistant to get it.

OFFICE GREETINGS

Although corporate cultures vary from business to business and even from region to region, the exchange of daily greetings is a ritual everywhere. Co-workers usually say hello first thing in the morning and then simply smile when they pass each other the rest of the day. No further verbal greeting is called for, and no one should take offense when a colleague doesn't stop to chat. It is considered rude, though, not to acknowledge fellow workers when you see them, even if it is for the fifteenth time in one day. You can nod or smile, but don't look the other way when you see someone.

Office Chitchat

Beyond routine greetings, how much people chitchat during the day generally depends on the atmosphere of the work environment. A formal, rigidly organized workplace may allow little room for casual conversation, while one that is informal and loosely organized leaves room for this kind of socializing. Sometimes talk is encouraged or discouraged by the nature of the work. An assembly line that involves heavy equipment or noise, for example, doesn't promote collegial chitchat, while an underworked sales staff may spend most of its work day talking.

In many workplaces, the chitchat—especially that of an extracurricular nature—is frowned on by management, and with good reason, since workers do have jobs to perform. Then the problem for an employee who wants to appear friendly is how to disengage from the friendly chatter without alienating co-workers.

When you must cut short a conversation to get to work, it helps to announce your reason in a friendly manner. For example, you might say, "I'd love to talk more, but I've got to finish the year-end budget report," or, "Can't talk right now. I have to finish these estimates."

If you disengage graciously, there should be no problem *except* for those relatively few workers who don't get the message. In these cases a little less friendliness is called for. Don't smile so broadly; don't stop to initiate a conversation. When a talker walks by, quickly say, "Hi there," but don't look up from your work expectantly. With time, she should get the message.

GETTING ALONG WITH THE BOSS

What bosses want is fairly simple. They want good employees—loyal, honest, hardworking team players, in a nutshell. Beyond this, what they expect in terms of deference is often more subtle and left to the employee to discern. The amount of deference bosses expect varies from office to office, but here are some general guidelines:

• Show respect by letting your boss go through doors and exit elevators ahead of you.

• Be slow to use first names. Until a boss tells you to call him "John" instead of "Mr. Leland," stick with the title, especially if you're young and newly hired. If the boss doesn't tell you what to call him, and you notice that everyone uses his first name, then after a few weeks or months on the job, you can switch to it, too.

• Let the boss take the lead in conversation. This doesn't mean you can never start a conversation or that you don't say good morning, just that most of the time you take your cue from her. In general, bosses get to set the tone, time, place, and content of your talks. It's presumptuous for a mailroom clerk (or almost any other employee) to take it upon himself to discuss golf, for example, with the chairman of the board while they're sharing an elevator.

WHAT MAKES A GOOD EMPLOYEE?

Here are ten simple rules that will make you beloved of bosses, fellow workers, and customers alike:

1. Be there when you're supposed to be. Show up on time and stay until quitting time. If you've ever called a business five minutes before closing and gotten an employee who'd already gone home mentally, you know what this is about. Stay on the job until it's time to leave.

2. Be dependable. If you say you'll do something, then do it. Others are counting on you.

3. Meet deadlines. Others may need your work before they can do theirs.

4. Be a team player. Don't go to the boss with every little criticism of a co-worker. All around, it's easier to work with others than against them, and workplaces should be team oriented.

5. Keep your private life out of the workplace as much as possible. Obviously you can't do this every minute, but it's still better to keep outside interference to a minimum.

6. Be courteous to everyone—the "small" people as well as the bigwigs.

7. Be fair to everyone. Treat everyone the same, regardless of gender, religion, race—or personality.

8. Respect others' privacy. Don't read a co-worker's mail or go through someone's desk unless it's absolutely necessary to do so.

9. Don't gossip. Sound like a funny rule for office life? Well, lots of offices are hotbeds of gossip, and lots of damage gets done. Good employees skip the gossip circuit.

10. Accept criticism graciously. Try to avoid taking it personally, and use it to improve your performance.

WHAT MAKES A GOOD BOSS?

It's up to employers and managers to initiate the kinds of relationships they want with their employees and also to set the tone for employees' behavior. If the bosses are rude or officious with customers, then employees will be, too. If bosses treat employees and customers with fairness and respect, this, too, will reverberate. Lots of bosses, though, aren't sure what's expected of them. Here are ten rules that will help a boss create a supportive atmosphere:

1. Take the lead. Bosses are supposed to set examples in all areas, from their work to their manners. Make sure you do this.

2. Show respect for all employees, regardless of gender, race, religion—or personality.

3. Respect employees' privacy. You may have to search an assistant's desk in his absence for a paper you need, and you certainly have the right to do so. But this doesn't give you the right to leaf through a checkbook or what is obviously personal correspondence.

4. Give frequent compliments and praise. People perform better and more efficiently when they are encouraged, and your job as the boss is to be the main encourager.

5. Make sure your criticism is fair. It's easier to accept graciously.

6. Respect others' autonomy. Put together a good team and then let them do their job. Infantilizing employees by looking over their shoulders at every move often makes for a belligerent, tense office environment.

7. Be available. If possible, leave your door open at least part of each day. Answer your own phone. Be open to ideas, even when they're critical of how you run things.

8. Use the name your employees prefer. If your female secretary is elderly, or even if not, use the appropriate title (Miss, Mrs., or Ms.). If a woman in your office marries but continues to use her maiden name, honor this.

9. Show small courtesies. You're the one with the power, thus it behooves you to extend small courtesies to make your employees more comfortable. When an employee comes into your office and needs to talk to you, ask her to sit down. When the employee leaves your office after a long talk, stand up to say good-bye. Shake hands and give a gracious welcome to an employee who's just returned from vacation or from some other absence.

10. Don't make employees your servants. Employees are there to work, not to do your every beckoning. Get your own coffee, balance your own checkbook, and do your own holiday shopping.

MAKING NEW EMPLOYEES FEEL WELCOME

The first day on a new job always feels strange. Only a rare person doesn't feel like an outsider in this situation. It's up to the old-timers to make the newcomer feel welcome in the work environment. The best bosses instigate a warm atmosphere by personally taking a new employee around to meet her fellow workers. A saintly boss even arranges a small—or large—lunch for a new employee or takes the new person to lunch alone.

Colleagues should try to put themselves in the newcomer's shoes and do what they can to make her feel comfortable. Shake hands and offer a warm, welcome-aboard greeting when you are introduced. Take some time to stop by during the day and find out how the newcomer is doing. If a new colleague asks where the ladies' room is, bring her there rather than simply pointing it out. This also gives you a chance to chat and begin to get to know one another. Try to include the new worker in any lunch plans, if you can. This is the most generous welcoming gesture of all. All offices are made up of cliques, and the new person may or may not settle into yours, but it doesn't hurt to socialize a little bit at the beginning in the interest of making someone feel comfortable in the new job.

OFFICE SOCIAL LIFE

Many offices are virtual beehives of social life, complete with their own patterns of gift giving, party schedules, and customs and traditions.

Collections

It is the custom in many offices to take up collections to buy presents for births, weddings, birthdays, and other happy occasions. Many people willingly participate in this tradition, but many more undoubtedly resent the continual expense.

Office collections only work among co-workers who genuinely have some fondness for one another and when the demands aren't too high. They don't work when you're in an enormous office and you barely recognize the person to whom you're expected to give money. They also don't work when a set amount, which is often beyond some people's means, is expected.

Asking people to kick in a dollar or two is okay. Asking for ten or twenty dollars usually is not. Those who know the person and want to give more always may, but no one should ever feel obliged to give more than a dollar or two to an office collection.

If you're taking up the collection, you can ease the situation by asking only those who really know the recipient to participate. Rather than exclude anyone, though, offer the choice to someone who may not want to contribute: "I'm taking up a collection to buy Mary a wedding gift, but I know you don't know her, so I don't feel it's right to ask you." That leaves the decision entirely in the hands of the giver. From the giver's point of view, once someone has let you off the hook in this way, you should feel no pressure to contribute. Another solution used in some offices is to pass around an envelope. Each person may anonymously contribute what he or she likes.

Office Parties

Another office tradition is giving parties to celebrate big events—baby showers, wedding showers, retirement parties, and the ubiquitous birthday parties. Strictly speaking, these ought not to be held on office time or premises, but they often are. Whenever possible, give major parties for co-workers at another location. Parties that take place at work, say, for a retirement or a birthday, should be kept fairly brief and subdued. Some large offices merge events—that is, they have one birthday party a month rather than a series of birthday celebrations.

Gifts

Most offices indulge in some form of gift giving, usually at holiday time. Bosses typically give gifts to their staff members, while employees are not obligated to give gifts in return. The exception is the secretary or personal assistant who wishes to give the boss a present. This gift can be very modest, even if the boss's gift was lavish. It would, in fact, be inappropriate for an employee to give an employer an elaborate or expensive gift.

Some offices have a grab bag gift exchange, where everyone puts his name in a bag and also draws the name of another worker. When these are the custom, the gifts should be small, and it is a good idea to set a dollar limit, usually five to ten dollars.

The best office gifts are impersonal but clearly chosen with an individual's interests in mind. Books, compact discs, food, desk accessories, datebooks, umbrellas, and impersonal items of clothing such as scarves and gloves are all acceptable. Joke gifts are fine and popular in many offices as long as they are not overly offensive.

Employers should also keep in mind that a bonus is not a present. It is part of the reimbursement package and as such should never be referred to or considered a present. Apart from any specific office rituals, gift exchanges among coworkers are the same as gift exchanges among friends. These are covered in Chapter 3 (see page 78).

MANAGING THE OFFICE ROMANCE

Now that so many women are in the workplace, men and women are more likely than ever before to meet and fall in love at work. Office relationships used to be frowned on and a pretty sure way for at least one party to the relationship—usually the woman—to get fired. But today, offices are much more accommodating, if only because they have little choice in the matter.

Bosses and co-workers do watch romantic liaisons with an eagle eye, no doubt partly out of voyeurism, but also to make sure the romance doesn't impair anyone's ability to function at work. So even the most torrid affair should be conducted with a decided sense of propriety. Here are some hints on accomplishing this:

• First and foremost, be discreet. Do this as much for yourselves as for those around you. Until you know a relationship will last, it is in your best interests to keep it as low key as possible.

• Don't arrive or leave together. Why give the wags ammunition?

• Don't flirt during the day or spend unnecessary time together. Couples shouldn't visibly court one another at work, nor should they huddle together on coffee breaks or at lunch. It makes too many people uncomfortable.

• Don't send each other cute messages via e-mail or fax. These aren't particularly private—and you're not only likely to be found out, you're also likely to become the butt of a lot of jokes.

These suggestions also apply to married couples who share a workplace, another increasingly common occurrence these days. You don't have to pretend you aren't married, and it's okay occasionally to pop into one another's offices for a quick conference about who is going to take Jennifer to her ballet class. But in general, the most successful couples, married or not, keep it strictly professional during the day.

When You Don't Want to Date a Co-Worker

One problem with the new acceptability of office romances is that it is harder not to date a co-worker when you prefer not to. There are two reasons a person may not want to become involved with a co-worker. One is the age-old adage about not mixing work and pleasure, and the other is a lack of interest in the individual who is asking. Both call for slightly different tactics.

In either situation, you must be kinder and let the person down more gently than you would if this were purely social. When you tell a casual or new acquaintance that you don't want to become involved, you usually don't see much of that person afterward. In an office setting, however, you still must see each other—and sometimes work together daily. Therefore it's imperative that you handle such situations with as much tact as you can muster.

It's easiest to say that you don't date co-workers. Explain that this isn't personal, it's just a rule you have. Put this way, a refusal will rarely hurt anyone's feelings for very long. However, if you think you might want to date a co-worker at some point, then you may want to leave the door open. In these situations it's often kinder to say you aren't available for a relationship right now.

Taking Rejection Politely

If you are on the receiving end of a rejection from a co-worker, it's polite to let the other person off easily, not least because you must continue your professional relationship.

Show respect for whatever reason the person gives you, and don't try to talk him or her out of it. You may think there's no reason not to date a co-worker, but that doesn't really matter in this particular situation. If your colleague feels this way, that's what matters.

Once you've made an overture and been turned down, let your co-worker make the next move if there is to be one. If the colleague later discovers he or she is interested in you or is free to date you, then it's up to that person to let you know. And of course, should the tables be turned at this point, he or she must respect your decision should you no longer be interested.

Finally, if the object of your affections does strike up an office romance with someone else at a later date, leave it alone. Of course you'll be disappointed, but these things happen. The all-important thing is to preserve the work relationship. Besides, did you really want to hear the true reason your colleague wasn't interested in dating you? It's far better to swallow any disappointment you may feel and let the work relationship proceed without animosity.

When an Office Romance Ends

People who engage in office romances occasionally have to deal with the pain of breaking up—and still see the person every day. When this happens, it's up to both of you to maintain a polite and professional demeanor. Don't tell your side of what happened around the office. Don't take it out on the person in meetings or in private. Treat each other as kindly as you can. Of course, if the pain is severe, you may want to look for another job—but that's a different issue.

Sexual Harassment

Unwanted sexual advances are terrible to deal with, especially when they come from someone with power over you. While both men and women are sexually harassed, it happens far less often to men. Until you're certain that you're being harassed, the best policy is firm politeness. Say "no" clearly, but say it politely.

If the person does not get the message and/or you sense that you're into the realm of sexual harassment, then this is one of the few occasions in life when politeness is no longer called for. You'll want to document the unwanted attentions and then report them to the proper person, either your boss or your boss's boss or personnel.

Sometimes sexual harassers genuinely do not understand what constitutes harassing behavior. For the record, in an office setting, it is never appropriate, let alone polite, to make an overt physical or verbal overture to a co-worker. Unacceptable gestures include touching, fondling, lewd comments, comments about someone's sexuality, even compliments that are phrased in a sexual way. Finally, but most important, when someone says "no," that means *no,* regardless of how softly or timidly it has been said.

THE OFFICE DRESS CODE

Every office has a dress code, but in today's casual workplace, they aren't always written. Instead it is up to each individual to figure out what's acceptable and what's not.

This actually makes it harder to dress appropriately, but fortunately most offices also send out a few signals.

Start by taking a cue from others. Does everyone wear conservative suits? Then you'd best follow suit, no pun intended. Are jeans and denim shirts the norm? Then it's okay to go casual, although you may want to dress up a little the first few weeks when the boss is sizing you up. This is especially true if the boss doesn't dress down as much as everyone else does.

Don't buck the system. The more conservative your workplace is, the riskier it is, in fact, to do this. Clothes are especially important in button-down environments, and while this may leave you chomping at the bit to reveal the real you, the risk usually isn't worthwhile.

Dress-Down Fridays

Since Americans love casual dress, it's surprising how many of us are at least mildly uncomfortable with the relatively new office custom of dress-down Fridays. People seem to be unsure how to interpret it. Plus, even dress-down days have their unwritten rules.

Many people want to know if they actually have to dress down. Some people are uncomfortable doing so or don't think they look their best in casual clothes. In this case the solution is to dress down a little but not a lot. Let's face it—a formal suit does stand out when everyone else is wearing sneakers and jeans, so you won't want to ignore the custom entirely. On the other hand, if you like how you look dressed up, then do a little of both. Wear jeans or casual pants and a nice shirt and a jacket or a blazer. This way you won't stand out, and you will still feel comfortable.

Don't err too far in the other direction, either. Nowhere do dress-down days mean that you can come to work in your grubbiest clothes. Some clothes are never meant to be seen by your fellow workers. Office casual typically means carefully tailored, well-made casual clothes. Leisure suits, sweats, or exercise clothes are best left at home—or in your locker at the gym.

Dressing up for Work

Dressing up for work can be just as hard as dressing down. Dressy office occasions include dinner with a client, dinner at the boss's house, a banquet, a client's party, or an office holiday party.

For women especially, dressy clothes for business occasions are not the same as dressy clothes for purely social occasions. For work-related events, it's better to skip the low-cut or slinky dress. Wearing it may forever change your image in ways you won't particularly like. Opt instead for conservatively cut clothes in conservative colors. Skip anything with frills or lace (except for a top under a suit)—and skip the bright red minidress.

SMOKING AND EATING AT WORK

Eating and smoking are the two most frequently cited problems in offices, and both can be handled easily with a dose of gracious manners.

Eating in the Office

There are two kinds of problems with food in the office. The first is with the problem eater—that is, the person who eats steadily and leaves a mess that others either have to look at or, worse, clean up. We're speaking of the kind of person who leaves banana peels in desk drawers until they rot—and the odor becomes a communal problem.

When the eater's mess spills over into other people's spaces, the best approach is a direct one. The only decision is whether to send an individual or a committee to talk to the offender. But the person should be told—tactfully and kindly—that the mess offends others. If all else fails, you can appeal to management, but it's less embarrassing if these matters can be worked out quietly.

If you're the eater, it may help to think about how your habit looks. Stale food and garbage, especially the kinds that smell, are not pleasant. Most helpful is to remove all food at the end of the day or put it in the garbage. If you use a communal refrigerator, clean out your food every few days. When you eat at your desk or in a lunchroom, clean up after yourself. Gather up all the wrappers and other papers, wipe up the crumbs, and remove the tray or any other items. Leave the table neat for the next person.

The other food problem that divides co-workers is dieting. Most of the time it's better not to bore your colleagues with your efforts to lose weight. But if you're seriously dieting, and you feel you need support at work, it may be worth discussing what you're doing. Just don't dwell on it. And don't expect your fellow workers to alter their eating habits for you.

If you're bothered when the snack cart comes around or don't think you can handle birthday cake, then absent yourself from the scene. Take a brief walk or run an errand in some other part of the building. It's up to you to move away from the food, not the other way around. If you've made yourself scarce during a birthday party or some other social occasion, be sure to drop by later to wish the celebrant well.

Conversely, if you know someone is dieting, try to be supportive. This generally means that you don't offer the dieter candy or other snacks continuously, and you don't, if possible, spend a lot of time talking about food. But there's also no need to be secretive about food or to keep it out of sight because someone is dieting. This is one of those situations where common sense should prevail.

Many people like to eat lunch at their desks, and this is fine. The only rule about this is to try to eat at a reasonably appropriate hour. If you are eating a meal, there is no need to offer to share it as you might a box of cookies.

Smoking in the Office

Smoking is trickier than food, largely because we seem to be in the midst of a war over it and, more important, because secondhand smoke is dangerous. As more and more offices become smoke-free, there will be fewer problems, but for now, smokers and nonsmokers must still coexist. At the moment, the burden seems to be on the smoker. Here are some hints to help smokers get along with everyone:

- Smoke only in designated areas.
- Never light up in someone's office without asking permission. If you don't see an ashtray, that's probably a hint that smoking is discouraged, if not banned.
- If you share an office or space with someone who can't tolerate smoke for whatever reason, one of you should request a new space. If this can't be worked out, then you must smoke elsewhere.

Finally, a word for nonsmokers: When you ask someone not to smoke, do it politely. Even better is to offer a word of support, perhaps by saying, "I hate to ask," or, "I know it's a pain. I'm a former smoker myself." At a minimum, this can help to defuse the situation. Smokers should not be harassed to give up smoking, either. It's impossible for any person not to know the dangers of this habit—and many smokers do want to quit—but they don't need to be reminded by either well-intended or belligerent colleagues.

ELEVATOR ETIQUETTE

Elevator etiquette, once very ritualistic, has become much less so in recent years—so many people no longer know what's expected of them. In times past, men doffed their hats upon entering an elevator and always let "ladies" leave the elevator first.

Today, few men have hats to doff and women don't necessarily leave first—unless they're the boss. In many workplaces, elevator etiquette is happily (and logically) egalitarian; whoever is in the front of the elevator exits first. But in others, a new kind of pecking order has replaced the old one. The new one is based on power and rank instead of gender. To wit:

• Executives get off before line staff. This means CEOs get off before midlevel managers, midlevel managers get off before mailroom clerks, and the chairman of the board gets off before everyone else.

• *Everyone* lets customers or clients get off first.

• If you're an egalitarian boss who isn't comfortable when everyone moves aside to let you exit first, you can motion for others to go ahead of you. But be warned that you may find it's easier to accept the perk than to buck the system.

• Now that so many women are in the workplace, and in positions equal (or superior) to men, they are no longer accorded automatic status based on their sex. This means if you're a woman and the boss, you get off first. If you're a woman and not the boss, you get off after the boss with everyone else.

There are still a few old-school gentlemen who can't stand not letting a "lady" get off first. And some women find such treatment condescending—a sort of reverse discrimination—while others don't mind. A gracious woman, no matter what her feelings about this treatment, probably does better not to argue when she's accorded these little courtesies, especially when they're offered by her boss. If you can find it in yourself to do so, simply say thank you and vow silently to fight the good fight on another battleground.

• One behavior everyone follows—or should: Make room for others. Whenever you enter an elevator, move to the back.

• If you're in the back of the elevator, others may not know that you want to get off. Simply say, "Excuse me," and people will step aside so you can exit the elevator.

• Well-mannered colleagues also honor the difference between a morning and an evening ride in an elevator. The difference, pure and simple, is caffeine. In the morning, before people have had their coffee or tea, a tactful co-worker doesn't start a conversation that requires much in return.

OFFICE COMMUNICATIONS: PHONE, MAIL, FAX, AND E-MAIL

Telephone

As your company's representative, your phone manners should be impeccable. Too many workers who are abrupt on the phone rationalize their behavior by saying it's okay—or even expected—since they're at work, but this isn't true.

You are putting across your company's image and should work just as hard at it on the phone as you would in person.

There are several accepted ways to answer a telephone at work. You can simply say "Hello" or you can say your name, as in "June Johnson speaking." You don't need to say the company's name if a receptionist or a secretary has already done so. Try to speak in a pleasant, unrushed voice. If you are rushed and can't talk, it's better to say this and make plans to call back later. Don't rustle papers or work while you're speaking on the phone. If you're really too distracted to speak, then reschedule the call.

It's okay and sometimes even necessary to screen your calls. But there is a right and a wrong way to do this. First train your secretary to do it politely. It's better to ask "May I say who's calling?" than "Who is this?" or even "Who's calling?" Second, don't instruct your secretary to say you are out when you are in. It's acceptable to be in but too busy to talk at the moment—and it's always better to be honest. Callers sense the difference, and besides, it may not look good if you're always out.

It's rude not to return telephone calls—regardless of whom they are from. You might be ignoring a potential customer. Many people today don't bother to return phone calls, and if you work for someone else, it's highly unlikely that such behavior is acceptable. When you do return calls, try to place them yourself. If you must have your secretary make the call, then get on the line immediately. It's not polite to keep someone waiting when you've placed the call.

Handling Mail

Good manners also dictate that you handle your mail promptly and courteously. Unless mail is obviously mass-produced, it should be deemed worthy of a reply. Simply burying work—an increasingly common custom, I'm con-vinced—catches up with most people sooner or later. Most bosses don't like discovering that their employees are unre-sponsive to business calls and letters.

Faxes and E-Mail

The arrival of fax machines and desktop computers in most offices has also given rise to a new etiquette regarding their use. Never assume that either a fax or e-mail is private. And with that in mind, never send any communication via either method that you wouldn't mind having your boss, or even your entire office, read. Most fax machines are located in public places, so anyone who passes by can read them, and some businesses routinely screen their employees' e-mail. (That's not necessarily polite, but it's easier to keep e-mail impersonal than to tell the boss she can't read it.)

BUSINESS ENTERTAINMENT

Many jobs extend to entertaining for business purposes. Even if this takes place after work hours, the company is the host and always foots the bill. As the host of business enter-tainment, you select the restaurant and also set the tone for ordering the food and drinks.

When your guests arrive, you may seat them where you please. Since this is a business dinner, seating arrangements may have more to do with any business you hope to conduct than with social arrangements.

The first order is usually to have drinks, if yours is a com-pany where drinking is not frowned upon. If you have a drink, your guest will usually feel free to have one; if you don't, your guest may not be so comfortable having one. In these days when increasing numbers don't drink, many people have learned how to make it comfortable for a guest to order a drink even if they don't plan to do so themselves. They say, "Let's have drinks," and then motion for their guest to order first. Or they might order a "light" drink—a wine spritzer is a good choice in this department—and then sip it.

At a business meal, guests will look to their host for clues even about what to order, and savvy hosts usually try to offer some. You can say, "The appetizers are wonderful here. And I love the fish for an entrée, but I've tasted almost everything on the menu, and it's all good." This accomplishes two things: it lets your guest know he should feel free to order anything on the menu, and it also gives him some genuine ideas about what food is best in a restaurant that may be new to him.

The self-consciousness about ordering at a business meal usually has less to do with the cost of the meal, since this is clearly an expense-account meal, and everything to do with figuring out how much time you will spend eating. It's embarrassing to order four courses when your host orders one.

The last subject that baffles many at a business lunch is when they can talk business. Most of us figure out something that works for us personally. But in general, it's more polite not to talk business during the meal, except in the most casual way. When coffee is served, you can haul out the papers and settle down to the serious discussion.

THE VAST MAJORITY OF OUR ENCOUNTERS WITH FELLOW workers are mundane. We greet one another in the morning or nod as we pass by each other several times a day. But even though these encounters are routine, when they're done in a kind and polite fashion, the payback can be enormous. All these little everyday courtesies that don't seem like much one by one, when taken together, add up to a congenial, pleasant work environment—and that's something everyone appreciates.

Chapter 5

PUBLIC LIFE

❋

ALTHOUGH IT IS EASY TO THINK THAT ONLY CELEBRITIES have public lives, the fact is that we're all in the public eye to some extent. We attend an array of events, such as lectures, movies, plays, and concerts. There is our community life, which encompasses our relationships with neighbors and acquaintances. We join churches and synagogues and other organizations. And we sit on committees and undertake other projects that cause us to interact with other people hundreds, if not thousands, of times each year. In all of these interactions, some with people we like a great deal (and some not), manners are an invaluable aid. In this chapter you will learn how to live your public life comfortably and graciously.

YOUR CHILDREN IN PUBLIC

Americans enjoy public outings, especially family outings. Children tend to eat at the table with their parents from an early age and are often taken to restaurants and other public places. These activities are more fun for everyone when children are well behaved. Parents need not make a fetish out of requiring good behavior of their children, but sensitivity to the feelings of others is essential.

Before taking your children out in public, especially for something as important as a meal in a nice restaurant, it is helpful to have a small dress rehearsal. At minimum, you should talk to them in advance about where you are going and what kind of behavior will be expected. Children are eager to please, and simply letting them know that certain things will be expected of them is often enough to put them on their best behavior.

Children should never be allowed to take over a public space by running noisily wherever they please with no restrictions. This is as much for their own safety as for the convenience of others. In a favorite museum, I often see four-year-olds running down hallways with very slick marble floors. Besides the shrieking, which is a bit too much for me, I worry that one of them will fall and be hurt—or that they will plow into a frail (or even not so frail) senior citizen.

That said, I would qualify the guideline by adding that children should be allowed to participate fully in public activities. And in the course of doing so, they will make some noise and create some flow of energy simply because they are children. Parents are obliged to *moderate* their children's activities and noise levels, not obliterate them.

As shocked as I am by parents who let their children run wild, I am also dismayed by those who seem to think children should never appear anywhere in public, and that if they do, they should never utter a sound. It is as rude to glare at a child's behavior as it is to glare at an adult's, and even people who are not fond of children should keep in mind that they are entitled to go out at certain times and to certain places.

Where Children Are Welcome in Public

One of the things all parents have to figure out is when and where their children are welcome. Some restaurants and hotels, for example, welcome children all the time, some not at all, and some only on what might be called the early shift (that is, before the evening rush hour).

These rules, of course, are rarely written but are a matter of social custom. They vary from community to community. Polite families abide by them, while impolite families take their children everywhere regardless of the place or the hour or whether the event is appealing to children. It is fair neither to others nor to the children themselves, who often end up unhappy and whiny through no fault of their own.

It is appropriate to take children to restaurants that welcome them or to take them early enough so they won't cause an uproar simply because they are exhausted. And look for hotels and resorts that cater to families: advertisements, word of mouth, and planned activities for children will tell you if the hotel is right for you.

You will find that your children will be welcome at parks, museums, sports outings, fairs, children's movies, and other events and places they will enjoy. However, it is not appropriate to take children—small children in particular—to such adult activities as concerts, plays, and movies with content that will bore them and therefore make them restless.

When I see children in inappropriate places, or out at an inappropriate hour, I do not fault the child so much as the parent. I understand that every moment with a child can be precious, especially these days when in many families both parents work. This prompts us to bring our children to places and events where we would not have taken them a few decades ago. But it is better for everyone if parents spend time with their children doing age-appropriate activities and then leave them home when they do something that really is geared to adults.

Dining out with Children

Parents who dine out with their children should take responsibility for how the children behave. Children should not be allowed to roam around the restaurant, where they could conceivably interfere with the service. They should also not be allowed to make a mess at the table; if they are too small to stop, the parents should make some effort to clean up the worst of it. If the staff indicates they would rather you not bother with this, then you are off the hook. Otherwise it is up to parents to pick up the large chunks of food and the four spoons dropped under the table and wipe up the big spills.

Going out When a Child Is Ill

Another phenomenon of our busy lives is that now we tend to be more casual about taking children out when they are ill. This may be unavoidable for a single parent or under certain circumstances, but in general, children (and adults, for that matter) belong at home when they are sick. It is thoughtless and rude to assume that your child is welcome anywhere with chicken pox or even a bad cold.

When Children Go out Alone

By the time youngsters reach their preteen years, they are old enough to go out alone. Well, not strictly speaking alone, but with their peers, which can be even more frightening. All parents should at least attempt to talk to their teens about what is acceptable behavior in public, to wit:

• Keep noise down in public. However much teens like calling attention to themselves, few other people appreciate it. Remind your child that it is rude to be excessively loud in public, especially in closed spaces such as buses or subways.

• Don't take over anything in public, be it the sidewalk, a bus, or a restaurant. Remind your teen not to walk four abreast on sidewalks or in malls.

• Be respectful to authority. Waiters, bus drivers, and anyone else who works in a public capacity deserves to be treated with politeness—even if they are not particularly polite back. Remind your children that serving the public can be a very difficult job—and rude customers do not make it any easier.

• Be respectful to the elderly. Well-mannered children are taught to offer their seats to the elderly, pregnant women, mothers with young children, and anyone else who might need them. I find it appalling to see a young person get on the bus and plop down on a seat while an older person stands struggling for balance. Ironically, I don't think this is as sad for the older person as it is for the child. There are quiet joys in doing something kind for another person, and children who are not taught even the rudiments of courteous behavior are deprived of one of life's more significant small pleasures.

We all know that teens are captive to their peer groups to a large extent, but a few gentle reminders, delivered in a nonpressured way, can help to instill a sense of appropriate behavior. One strategy for doing this is not to criticize your own child's behavior, but rather to point out, in a low-key manner, some problems with the behavior of other teens when you observe it. You can also encourage your child to be a leader—that is, to be the one in his group who offers his seat to an elderly person.

DAY CARE COURTESIES

Millions of children now attend day care, yet day care centers have sprung up rather haphazardly—and so has the etiquette surrounding them. Day caretakers are not quite accorded the status of teachers, but neither are they on a level with baby-sitters and cleaning people. Most of us, in fact, aren't quite sure what is expected of us regarding our child's caretakers.

For a start, basic courtesy and consideration go a long way. And in this department the most important, and most widely disregarded, rule, is this: Do not arrive early to drop off your children or late to pick them up. Day care centers have hours when they are open and regular closing times, and parents should respect these. It is acceptable (or at least sometimes understandable) to occasionally call an at-home baby-sitter and ask her to stay late, for additional pay, but it is not acceptable to do this to day caretakers.

Day care workers do have other lives, and equally important, they are salaried employees—ones who might even have some children of their own to pick up somewhere. Day caretakers are like teachers in that they are entitled to set hours—and parents who violate those hours are thoughtless. If you do ask a day caretaker to do something extra, expect to pay for it—either by the hour or, if money is declined, with an appropriate small gift.

A single mother I know does sometimes have to arrive late to pick up her child, but she has worked out a special arrangement with one of her son's caretakers. She pays for his and her son's dinner, and the caretaker takes the child out for several hours and then meets her back at the day care center at a designated time. When he declined any hourly pay beyond the cost of his dinner, she began buying him gift passes to his local movie theater—a payment he loves because he has a limited budget and he finds it much easier to accept than money.

The other major day care offense is not keeping sick children at home. All working parents should have a backup plan, and if a day care center does not have its own contingency plans for dealing with sick children, then the parent's backup plan should be activated. Never should children be sent to day care when they are ill. If you are in doubt, contact the day care center for advice.

Gifts, of course, are appreciated at holiday time. However, educators and caretakers get more than their share of gifts they do not need and cannot use. So smart parents give gift certificates, subscriptions, and gourmet foods. These are admittedly impersonal, but they are generally welcome. If at all possible, find out what people's interests are and try to give appropriate gifts.

GETTING ALONG WITH YOUR CHILD'S TEACHER

There is also an art—and an etiquette—to getting along with your child's teachers. Every parent should start by respecting the teacher's professionalism. Too often parents assume their child is right and the teacher is wrong when, in fact, parent and teacher should work as a team to ensure the best possible educational experience for the child. Apart from that, here are a few hints that will help to make this an easygoing, cordial relationship:

- Call the teacher "Mr.," "Miss," or "Ms." until told otherwise or unless it absolutely is the style of the school to be informal. (Note that it is the style of the school and not your personal style that should prevail here.) This goes double for the principal and other school administrators.
- Make appointments to discuss your child. It is rude to call and simply expect a teacher to be available at any time.
- Make an effort to get to know your child's teachers. A teacher does not have to become your close friend, but a little camaraderie goes a long way.
- When you must express a criticism, do so fairly and in a low-key way. Always keep in mind that this person will be spending many months with your child, and it behooves you to maintain cordial ties the entire time. This is not to say that you should be cowed or not speak up about something that is troubling, but you should do so with the respect an educator deserves.
- Invite the teacher to your home for dinner if this appears to be a desirable thing to do. If your child expresses an interest in entertaining a teacher, or if the teacher himself seems open to this, a dinner invitation—and a chance for you all to get to know one another better—may be very welcome.
- Do not invite the teacher to your home if this appears to be inconvenient. A teacher who is frazzled (by an unusually large class load, for example), or who is attending night school, or who commutes many miles to and from work, may not appreciate an invitation. Use some sensitivity in these matters. (This kind of socializing occurs far more frequently in small towns and cities than in large urban areas.)
- Extend favors to your child's teacher when you can. If you find yourself with play or concert tickets you cannot use, it is a nice gesture to offer them to your child's teacher if they are something that will be of interest.

- Buy your child's teacher a small gift at holiday time. Since teachers do not usually give their students presents, this is an excellent opportunity to teach your child how to give without expecting anything in return.

- When buying a teacher's present, avoid the obvious such as perfume and scarves. If you know a teacher's tastes, books and compact discs are acceptable. Otherwise stick to gift certificates, edibles, and subscriptions.

GETTING ALONG WITH THE NEIGHBORS

Neighbors may or may not become our best friends, but there is a definite art—and an etiquette—to getting along with them. Perhaps nowhere else does the Golden Rule do more to help people get along.

In a nutshell, this means if you would not like to hear your neighbor blasting music at 11 P.M. because you are usually in bed at that hour, then you in turn do not mow your lawn at 7 A.M. just because you happen to be up and energetic at that hour. Across America, in communities of all sizes and forms, the noise level goes down around 10 P.M. and by mutual agreement does not go up again until around 8 A.M., perhaps even 9 or 9:30 A.M. on weekends.

Never assume that any part of your neighbor's property is yours. If you have a tree that drops leaves on a neighbor's yard, ask if you can remove the leaves—or, better yet, if she would like the tree trimmed so this does not happen. More neighborly disputes occur over property disagreements than anything else.

It is also polite to inform your neighbors when you will be undertaking a construction project. They will be less likely to resent the noise and the mess if they know about it in advance, know what it entails, and, most important, know when it will end. Apologize for any inconvenience—and if there truly has been some, think about doing something to make amends.

Sometimes the way to make amends is obvious. If you just wreaked havoc putting in a swimming pool, then the neighbors who were inconvenienced should be among the first people invited to enjoy the fruits of their discomfort. Alternately, you might send over a couple of bottles of wine or even a case, depending upon how sizable the inconvenience was. And of course, it goes without saying that if so much as a zinnia plant is disrupted by your endeavors, it should be promptly replaced.

If a dispute does arise, try to settle it promptly and personally. Few things are sadder than two families living next door to each other in a state of animosity. This happens only because people let it happen. When a conflict does arise, good neighbors settle it quickly and amiably.

I recently had cause to complain about a neighbor's puppy who raced through my new rosebed and destroyed several plants. I thought of writing a note but decided the informal, personal touch might work better since although we were on friendly terms, my neighbors were new to our community. So I paid a call, and after a bit of polite chitchat I described what had happened in a calm, nonconfrontational voice. I was assured the dog would be leashed in the future, and an offer was made to replace the roses, which I declined because no real damage had been done.

When I saw my neighbors the next time, I made sure to walk over to say hello because I did not want any ill feelings to grow up after the fact. I even went so far as to rub the head of the little culprit (toward whom I was not yet feeling all that friendly). And as a sort of coup de grace, on the day my roses bloomed, I delivered three perfect ones to my neighbors. I wanted to reinforce what could happen if the puppy were kept away from my flowers, which he diligently was from that time on. This predicament ended well, but it is exactly the kind of occurrence that can easily go the other way, engendering months, if not years, of hard feelings.

Finally, it is important to realize that while you do not have to be best friends with your neighbors, it is to everyone's benefit to maintain good congenial relations. The fact is that it's simply easier to live in harmony. Fortunately, this can be accomplished with old-fashioned common sense mixed in with a heavy dose of consideration.

Maintaining Reasonable Boundaries

It is also acceptable to maintain certain boundaries where your neighbors are concerned. Some people feel comfortable having neighbors in and out of their homes all the time—and some do not. You may feel hurt by neighbors who have no intention of getting to know you, or you may feel relieved. In any event it is up to you and your neighbors to work out the kind of relationship that everyone enjoys. Keep in mind, though, that it is probably easier to melt the unfriendly neighbor than to undo the overly friendly relationship once it is established.

Most of us veer away from people who are too eager to be friendly, but sometimes these people simply do not take a hint. In such situations it is helpful to know what is and is not expected of you. You should say hello or wave as you come and go, but you need not feel obligated to stop and talk, and indeed it may not be wise to do this with someone who is pressing in on you too closely.

More important, you are always entitled not to be "at home" even when you are in your house. If someone telephones at a bad time, politely let them know this is an inconvenient time, then offer to call them back. Similarly, if someone shows up at your door, explain that this is a bad time and schedule another visit (or say you will get back to them). Or you can simply not answer the door. Obviously you cannot sit within eyesight of someone and pretend to see nothing, but if you are inside the house and out of sight, it is always up to you whether or not you want to answer the door.

If the neighbor complains about your lack of response (and the busybodies usually do), casually say, "Oh, I was at home, but I was on the phone [or listening to music or bathing the baby] and couldn't answer the door right then. It would be better if you called me rather than dropping by." Most people will take this rather broad hint.

Ultimately, of course, instead of backing away from a neighborly relationship that is threatening to engulf you, it is better not to let it get out of hand in the first place. Many people tend to test the boundaries when they are becoming acquainted. You can usually see when someone is on your wavelength in terms of how much time you want to spend with them or how much privacy you require. This is the point at which to establish the limits that will make you comfortable.

Greeting New Neighbors

Even twenty years ago there was a ritualistic way to get to know the new neighbors. Someone, meaning the wife, baked some kind of dessert and delivered it to the newcomer's doorstep. Because the dish in which the dessert was baked was real, it had to be returned, and it always was, along with an invitation for coffee or cocktails. Thus it was that two couples began the process of figuring out just how friendly they wanted to be with one another. No one risked an entire evening at first, and no one was obligated beyond the two gestures.

These days, with so many women working, we are lucky if we even lay eyes on our new neighbors for the first few months they live near us. Busy or not, the neighborly thing to do is to greet newcomers, even from afar, as soon as you notice them. It is no longer customary to ask them over, but it is polite to walk over and introduce yourself at some point. This invariably leads to at least some conversation, which in turn points up what you may—or may not—have in common. From this simple gesture a friendship arises, if indeed friendship is in the stars.

In urban areas, where most people live in apartments, greeting customs are slightly different. Once you recognize someone as a neighbor, it is appropriate to offer a friendly acknowledgment when you pass each other, but you are under no obligation to ask a neighbor to your home.

Breaking the Ice in a New Community

If you are the newcomer to a community, you may be more eager than your neighbors to make connections. Obviously, waiting for others to make the first move can backfire, because everyone is so busy. So what can you do? In these circumstances you may have to put yourself forward to get acquainted. Here's how to go about it:

• You make the first move. If you have been saying hello to a neighbor or someone you see somewhere else (when you drop off your child at day care, for example), then introduce yourself and suggest a play date for your children or a quick cup of coffee someday before you pick them up.

• Walk over and introduce yourself to your neighbors rather than waiting for them to introduce themselves to you. In cities it is helpful to have a reason to introduce yourself, but even a fairly flimsy pretext will work. The fact that your children have met or that you both own dogs will suffice.

• Attend public meetings and other events and make a point of speaking to people, generally letting it be known that you are new in town.

• Ask questions—people like to give advice. Inquiring about where the farmer's market is or who is a good veterinarian are good icebreakers.

Once people see that you are friendly, you will be asked to serve on committees and otherwise get involved in community life.

COMMUNITY LIFE

Sooner or later you will become involved in one or another community activity, usually through your child's school or some social, religious, or charitable organization.

If you do volunteer work, make sure you do it as well as you can. Expect to work with others, including people you don't like. Arrive on time and be prepared at all meetings. Groups trying to accomplish something take enough time without also being weighed down with a perennial late arrival or someone who does not bother to do his share.

If you will be conducting meetings, buy yourself a copy of *Robert's Rules of Order,* a wonderful little book that explains the rules of parliamentary behavior and makes all meetings hum along smoothly. You need not follow every rule, but it helps to understand the overall procedure.

When you have had enough of public life for a while, and most of us reach this point every so often, bow out graciously. When someone calls you to work on a project, simply explain that you are taking some time off. Then, when you are ready to jump back in, raise your hand to volunteer or pass the word.

PATRIOTISM

Patriotism can be exhibited in many ways, but the most frequent one is to fly the American flag. And for that, it is important to know flag etiquette:

- The flag should be flown only during daylight hours.
- It should never be flown in inclement weather.
- On Memorial Day the flag is flown at half-staff until noon, then hoisted to full staff. Apart from that, it is flown at half-mast only in times of national mourning, never for our own personal purposes.
- When a flag is flown at half-mast, it is hoisted to the top of the flagpole briefly before being lowered. It is raised to the top again before it is lowered for the day.
- The flag should be raised briskly and lowered slowly and solemnly.
- When displaying the flag vertically, the Union (the blue field) is placed to the north on an east-west street and to the east on a north-south street.
- When a flag is displayed from a window or against a wall, the Union goes to the left of the observers.
- A flag is never hung upside down except to signal distress.
- The flag should never be used to drape anything. For example, it should never cover a statue or a speaker's table.
- The flag should not touch the ground, water, or the the floor.
- Flags should never be flown when tattered, torn, or dirty.

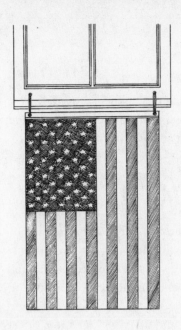

DISPLAY OF FLAG FROM A WINDOW

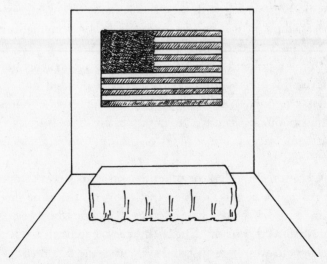

DISPLAY OF FLAG AGAINST A WALL

PUBLIC ACTIVITIES

We engage in many "public" activities, from movies to plays to concerts to dining out with friends. Here is how to finesse each with an ease that will make you popular wherever you go.

Line Etiquette

The first and perhaps only important rule of lines is to know your place, literally. Do not get in line in front of others. If you are not sure where a line begins and ends, ask. If you are not sure whether someone else is in line ahead of you, ask.

I once had acquaintances who arrived at the last minute at movie theaters and after buying their tickets did not get in line with the rest of us. Instead they stood near the front of the line, and when the line began to move, they simply eased into the theater ahead of almost everyone else. They saw nothing wrong with their behavior, while I (and several others) thought it showed an utter lack of communal spirit.

Should you encounter line jumpers, always try to deal with them politely. Sometimes people do accidentally get in line in front of others, and once this is pointed out, they quickly remove themselves. If someone jumps into a line in front of you, say calmly: "Excuse me, but I don't think that was your place in line." Most of the time the offender will back down.

Occasionally a clerk or other person who serves the public makes the mistake. When that happens, the same direct, calm approach works. Say: "Excuse me, but I believe I was here before this man." Often the clerk genuinely does not know who was there first and welcomes the comment. The situation is usually defused.

Movies, Plays, Dance, and Concerts

Only a few simple rules need to be followed to make public entertainments a pleasure for everyone. The first: Be prompt. It is rude not to be in your seat and ready when the performance begins. No one likes to settle into a movie or, worse, a play or a concert, only to be interrupted by late arrivals. In many places latecomers are not seated until an appropriate break. But even if this is not a house rule, you still show a great kindness to your fellow audience members by waiting for an appropriate break during which you can be seated.

It is acceptable to save seats in a movie theater. However, it is not acceptable to say that seats are taken when they are not so you can have a place to put your belongings. At concerts and plays, fortunately, seats are usually reserved. When they are not, the same rules apply as for movies.

If you are choosing a seat in an uncrowded theater or hall, it is polite not to sit right in front of other people or right next to them. A friend who once lived in Denmark reported that people there sometimes sit in one big cluster in movie theaters to fight off the chill. But Americans have central heat and like (no, make that *love*) their personal space, so do not sit next to others unless you have to.

When you enter a row of seats and must pass in front of someone who is already there, say, "Excuse me," to those whom you pass. If you are the seated person, it is especially polite to stand and even to move out into the aisle so that others can pass easily to their seats. And if you must leave while an event is in progress, whisper, "Excuse me," as you pass in front of others. As a point of interest, most Americans pass by people with their backs to them, while Europeans face the people they are passing.

Talking is never appropriate once a performance has begun. Although most people know enough to be quiet during plays and concerts, many seem to confuse movies with television—and thus think they can talk during the show. Some purists want all chat to stop during the previews, but everyone agrees that by the time the film's music swells and the credits begin to roll, the audience should be settled and silent. At a play, all talk should stop when the lights dim or when the performance begins, whichever comes first. At a concert, talk and applause stops when the conductor steps onto the podium.

If someone talks inappropriately after a performance has begun, it is acceptable to turn around and pleasantly (and quietly) ask him please to be quiet. If he does not comply, get up and inform management. It is then their problem to handle.

Many people enjoy watching the end credits run after a movie is over. It is polite to let them do this. You need not sit in your seat if you are not interested, but move out of it quickly and do not stand so that you are blocking someone's line of vision.

Applause

Applause is expected at various points during performances. People should always applaud at the end of a live performance. It is the players' reward and one they should not be deprived of. You need not stay for the last gasp of adulation, but neither is it polite to hustle your way out of the theater or concert hall the second a performance is over, especially if you have to pass by others to do this.

Occasionally, when a performance has been superb, a standing ovation is accorded the performers. It is the highest tribute they can receive. Once this has begun, it is fruitless to resist. Even if you do not feel a performance warrants it, you will not be able to see anything if you do not participate.

Standing ovations, as well as lengthy applause, often lead to encores, at least at musical performances. Invariably everyone in the audience sits back down for another ten or fifteen minutes of playing. But if you have a baby-sitter waiting or some other reason you must leave, then you may do so before the encore. And certainly once the first encore is over, you may slip out at any time during a break.

There are other times when applause is expected. At a play, the first round of applause sometimes occurs when the curtain goes up, as well as at the end of each act and, of course, at the end of the play. People also applaud the set and the appearance of stars, although the latter should be discouraged because it can interfere with the actors' lines.

At the ballet, viewers applaud at the end of every movement, at the end of each act if the ballet is divided into acts, and at the end of the performance. There is a growing trend to applaud the appearance of stars and riffs of spectacular dancing while they are still being danced, but this, too, should be avoided because it can interfere with the dance performance.

The greatest degree of silence is expected at live musical performances. Even rustling in your seat will draw frowns from those around you. You should never eat, suck candy, leaf through your program, tap your fingers, or move your legs or any body parts in time to the music. Do not applaud during the brief breaks between movements. Applaud only at the end of an act and at the end of the piece. If you are in doubt as to when this is, wait for others around you to initiate the applause or take a cue from the conductor, who will turn around to face the audience.

Coughing, Sneezing . . .

Think twice before attending a performance if you are ill. If you are well enough to attend, but still ailing, try sucking very quietly on a throat lozenge. If this fails and you suffer a fit of coughing, the only appropriate thing to do is to leave the performance so it is not ruined for others. You can return to your seat during the next break.

DINING OUT

In recent years, the number of Americans who dine in public has gone up enormously. I am not speaking here of the casual, caught-on-the-run meal, but rather of the meal that is itself entertainment. The fine points of table manners are covered in Chapter 7, but there is still a more general etiquette regarding this social custom.

Reservations

Many restaurants require reservations, which should then be honored with your prompt arrival at the appointed time. (In return, the restaurant should seat you within five to ten minutes after you arrive.) If you make a reservation and cannot honor it, it is polite to let the restaurant know. People have become so derelict about this that many restaurants now require guests to confirm their reservations within a specified amount of time.

Seating

Upon arriving, wait for the host or hostess to seat you. Women follow the maître d'hôtel, and men follow women.

(Even without a host, women walk ahead of men, although a man who is hosting a dinner may, in the absence of a maître d', walk ahead of his guests.) If the table is acceptable, seating begins. If it is not, it is entirely proper to ask the maître d' for another one.

At the table, the maître d' will offer the best seat to a woman or guest of honor. She sits down in it immediately, although if she prefers another seat, she may ask for it, or she may demur and offer it to her guest of honor or to an older person of either sex. If there is no maître d', the man hosting the party may hold a chair for one woman, and the other men may follow suit. Among younger people, this admittedly nonegalitarian gesture is often omitted. The host and hostess at a restaurant meal also may suggest where they would like their guests to sit. The host and hostess usually sit opposite each other, with their guests around them.

Ordering

The waiter often indicates the sequence in which he would like to take orders. He may prefer to take the women first, or (more often these days) he will work his way around the table regardless of gender. A good guest is ready with his order and rarely changes his mind—certainly never more than once.

Ordering Wine

Many restaurants serve wine by the glass, and in a good restaurant you will also be presented with a wine list. Lots of people feel intimidated by wine lists, but there is no reason to be.

If ordering by the glass, you may simply ask for a red or a white wine, or even a "dry" red or white. Alternatively, you may ask what wines are offered at the bar. If you aren't familiar with the varieties or labels the waiter names (there are literally thousands of wines), it's perfectly acceptable to ask the waiter which wine is driest or sweetest or whatever you prefer.

Most intimidating is the wine list and the ritual that surrounds it. However, even this is easily handled if you're willing to own up to the fact that you aren't a wine expert. Of course, if you are an expert, you may not need the waiter's or the wine steward's advice. But most of us need a consultation before ordering a bottle of wine. And many connoisseurs enjoy the consultation as well.

But first things first: It is perfectly appropriate to ask for the wine list and then, upon looking at it, to decide you do not want to order a bottle. You simply may not feel like drinking, or you may not feel like paying the asking price.

If you do decide to order wine, you may need advice on selecting something that will complement everyone's meals. Mention generally—or specifically—what you are having and then ask the waiter to suggest something. By the way, it is no longer the province of the man to order wine. If there is a woman present who knows something about it, it is perfectly appropriate for her to consult with the wine steward and make the final selection.

When the wine arrives, the bottle will be shown to the person who ordered it. It is a courtesy to waive the bottle without taking too close a look. But do at least glance at it to make sure that you have indeed gotten the wine—and the vintage—you ordered. The wine steward will then open the wine and pour a small amount in the glass of the person who ordered. He or she takes a sip and, assuming the wine is okay, passes on it so the waiter can fill the other glasses.

The reason for the tasting is to ensure that the wine is drinkable—that is, not spoiled. But the great contradiction in this custom is that only very rarely is a bottle of wine bad. Ironically, the older, high-priced bottle of wine is more likely to be bad than the $15–$30 bottle most of us tend to order. Therefore, once you have taken a sip of the wine and approved it, you can ask the waiter to serve everyone else at the table.

If the wine is white, it will be placed in an ice bucket. If it is red, it will be set on the table. The waiter should come back periodically to refill the wineglasses, but diners may also refill their own, as more wine is needed.

A bottle of wine provides four to six glasses, depending upon the size of the wineglass. Four diners who are drinking conservatively can share one bottle; otherwise, estimate accordingly (number of diners and their capacity) and order additional bottles as required.

Complaining

If something is not as ordered, it is entirely appropriate to send it back after describing the problem quietly and politely to the waiter. If the waiter takes a plate back, insist that your fellow diners begin their meals or continue eating—and they should indeed feel free to do this if their food is hot. If the food is cold, it is their choice whether they wait for you or go ahead.

Getting the Bill

When you are ready for the bill, you must ask for it. A good waiter usually will not deliver a bill unless requested. Look it over quickly to be sure it is correct. If it is, put out money or a credit card, and the waiter will take it away. If there is a problem, confer quietly with the waiter to fix it.

The presentation of the bill often incites an awkward moment over who will pay. Many people now share the bill when they eat out with friends. I think this makes for a neat division of expenses and helps to avoid any hurt feelings in the long run. However, if you plan to take out a couple or a group of friends, you should make this clear when the invitation is extended.

Any negotiating over the bill should be done quickly and quietly. The person who wants to buy mentions that she would like the other diners to be her guests. The others either accept and indicate that they will pay the next time or they decline. Some people really do not want to be obligated in this way, and these feelings should be respected.

Under no circumstances should a loud argument erupt, nor should the waiter be held hostage or involved in the discussion. Finally, keep in mind that in an increasing number of restaurants it is possible to ask the waiter to split the tab between two credit cards—a neat and tidy solution for all concerned.

Tipping

In most restaurants a tip of between 15 and 20 percent is expected. Fifteen percent suffices almost everywhere except in a very fancy restaurant, where you are waited on by both a captain and a waiter. The extra 5 percent goes to the captain or head waiter (not to be confused with the host, who merely walks you to your table and is not usually tipped). You need not divide the tip on the bill; the people who wait on you will do this later among themselves. If a wine steward has helped you, the extra 5 percent would go to her. If there is both a wine steward and a captain, or if the wine steward has given you serious assistance, then you may want to tip her separately—about 5–10 percent of the cost of the bottle. The coat check person should be tipped $1–$2, and the assistant in the rest room should be given $.50 to $1, depending upon how generous you feel and the degree of service that is rendered.

APPROPRIATE DRESS

It is sometimes difficult to know what to wear, especially when one is attending a party or performance in a new community. It is helpful to ask what kind of dress is appropriate. If you cannot do this, your best option is to dress down rather than up.

It is hard for a man to go wrong wearing a dark suit, whether he is at a casual dinner or an event that turns out to be black tie. Similarly, a woman in a simple dress or suit can hardly go wrong. For women, such outfits have an added advantage in that they can be dressed up or down with jewelry and other accessories.

HELPING HANDICAPPED PEOPLE

Few of us are totally comfortable about when or how to help a handicapped person. Not many years ago good manners would have dictated that we offer assistance, but this is not necessarily the case today. Handicapped people, who have waged their own battles over the issue of equal access to public places, tend to be both better able to take care of themselves and much more independent about doing so. The last few times I have offered assistance, I have been turned down, and I no longer routinely offer such help.

Even if handicapped people don't need assistance, however, we should be aware of extra courtesies that can be extended—the kinds of courtesies we should extend to one another anyway. I'm speaking of such things as holding a door open for someone, stooping to pick up a package that has been dropped, and offering a seat on public transportation.

When handicapped people do accept help, they usually have some feelings about how it is delivered. Blind people, for example, would rather take your arm than be steered by you. Remember too that helping someone doesn't give you a license to discuss his or her disability. Most handicapped people prefer to be treated just like everyone else, and we should strive to do just that.

CELLULAR PHONES

Cellular phones have proliferated to the point of being a nuisance. If you have one, think about turning it off in certain public places. A telephone should never be used in a restaurant or movie theater or during any kind of live performance. In fact, a phone should not be used in any public place where quiet is valued—and this includes parks.

APPROPRIATE BEHAVIOR EVERYWHERE

How we act in public says a lot about us, and how we act to the people who serve us is an even stronger test of our character. It is all too easy to be nasty to a waiter or someone who is essentially at our mercy. For this reason (among others) we should always be especially polite to those who serve us in public places. This involves a friendly smile and saying "please" and "thank you."

Feeling superior to others, whether in our public or private lives, undermines what good manners are all about. Truly gracious people—the kind most of us aspire to be—make a point of being gracious to everyone all the time. That's what being polite really means.

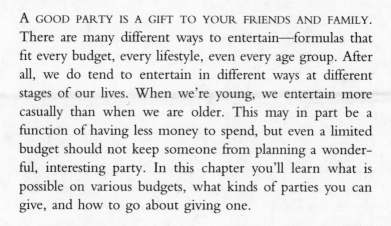

Chapter 6

ENTERTAINING

A GOOD PARTY IS A GIFT TO YOUR FRIENDS AND FAMILY. There are many different ways to entertain—formulas that fit every budget, every lifestyle, even every age group. After all, we do tend to entertain in different ways at different stages of our lives. When we're young, we entertain more casually than when we are older. This may in part be a function of having less money to spend, but even a limited budget should not keep someone from planning a wonderful, interesting party. In this chapter you'll learn what is possible on various budgets, what kinds of parties you can give, and how to go about giving one.

TAKING THE PLUNGE—THROWING A PARTY

The best way to learn how to give a party is to give a party. Going through the steps enables you to discover how much fun—and how rewarding—entertaining is.

Before you start, though, you should realize that parties are work, and they require considerable planning. I've known a few marvelous hostesses who were able to throw together incredible parties on a moment's notice, but this is, I believe, the exception. Most forms of entertainment require time, forethought, and quite a bit of elbow work.

Reasons to Give a Party

One of the most important things to know about a party is why you are giving it. If it's to introduce friends to one another, you may favor a small dinner party so two friends can really get acquainted. Alternatively, you may want a large, busy party if you are introducing not just two friends, but two or more groups of friends.

Some people entertain to make or strengthen business connections—to network, in other words. Many a business relationship has been cemented over a good dinner or some other form of entertainment that lets everyone get to know one another not only better, but in a completely different setting.

Parties are also planned around people and events: birthdays, anniversaries, Christmas, New Year's, a big football game, the spring equinox—whatever suits your fancy. Virtually any event offers an excuse to entertain.

Finally, a party may be a payback—a way to entertain those who have entertained you. Although the rules about this are not as strict as they once were, if someone has entertained you, you generally owe them a return invitation in one form or another. (Years ago you would have been expected to return the invitation in kind.)

In fact, there aren't many excuses for not entertaining. Single people used to be let off the hook, but not anymore. Now they are expected to entertain and to return invitations just like couples. Or are you waiting until your house is perfectly decorated? In these days of casual entertaining, that's no excuse, either.

I know one innovative hostess who threw a splendid party by serving a boiled lobster dinner on packing crates in her new home. She was forced to use paper napkins, which were better with the lobster anyway. Because she bought them at the last minute, they featured a theme more suitable for five-year-olds than forty-year-olds, which her guests found highly amusing. She put candles in wine and beer bottles since she hadn't yet unpacked any candle holders. The atmosphere was great and casual in a way that set everyone talking about some wonderful, heartwarming moments in their lives. It was a long and pleasantly drawn out evening and altogether memorable despite (or even because of) its modest circumstances.

FORMAL VS. INFORMAL ENTERTAINING

Most of the time we won't be entertaining in so casual a fashion. On the other hand, few of us give ultraformal dinner parties, either. Still, once in a while it's a great experience to stretch yourself to entertain if not in a truly formal manner, then at least in grand style.

The days of really formal entertaining—with gloved waiters, double service, five courses, four wines (including sherry and champagne), and guests wearing black tie or white tie—are, for the most part, gone. But this doesn't mean we can't entertain with flair and style. Even when a party is casual, the successful hosts will plan in advance. They'll do everything they can to make things as beautiful, as witty, or as clever as possible.

PLANNING THE PARTY

The first step is to put your plans in writing. It helps you focus on everything that must be done and then do it in a coordinated fashion. Many hostesses I know keep a notebook that they use especially for entertaining. In it they write the time and date of the party, the guest list, the foods and beverages that are served, and, correspondingly, how much they need to buy. Some hostesses also describe the linens, flatware, dishes, glasses, and, most especially, the service flatware and dishes they will use.

This record helps in two ways. First, it lets you calculate the cost before you start spending for the party. When you see on paper that you are planning to serve shrimp as an appetizer and filet mignon as a main course, you will realize that this will be an especially expensive party. You may, depending upon the size of your purse, decide to scale it down in one way or another. Second, the notes serve as a reference for future parties. You will know whom you invited and what you served, and in that way you can avoid repeating the same menu with the same people.

Inviting Your Guests

The next step is to rough out—and then finalize—a guest list. If a party is large, you need not worry too much about whether your guests are enormously compatible, although this always matters to some extent. But if it is small, inviting people who have nothing in common or who won't particularly enjoy one another's company can be the kiss of death. Granted, it is also up to your guests to get along and be gracious to each other, but you should still use your own instincts to produce a good mix of company.

I am often asked what can be done when two friends or, more usually, two relatives, don't get along well enough to be invited to the same party. If the party is small, it may be in your best interests to entertain the feuding parties separately. At large parties, especially where family is involved, you should feel free to invite both of them. Make it clear that this is what you are doing, and then let the warring parties decide whether to come and behave or decline the invitation entirely. These are, by the way, their only two options. Coming to the party and in any way spreading around their bad feelings is very bad manners.

Oral vs. Written Invitations

Most invitations these days are extended by telephone. In fact, a printed invitation usually signals a large party for a birthday, a shower, or some other special event.

Plan to call two to three weeks in advance for a big event, in less time for a smaller, last minute party. If you are extending a last minute invitation for whatever reason, it's tactful to offer a word of explanation, so your guest doesn't feel as if *he* alone is being invited at the last minute, possibly after someone on the A-list has declined your invitation. You might say, "Bill and I just decided to invite some friends over this weekend for a cookout. We know it's last minute, but we hope you'll be able to come."

When an invitation is extended by telephone, you may even get an immediate response. This isn't always the case, though, since anyone you invite has a right to tell you he has to check his calendar and call you back. He should, however, get back to you as soon as possible, preferably within a day or two after the invitation is extended.

Telephone invitations are acceptable for informal dinner

parties—even sit-down ones; drinks; coffee and dessert; and casual, medium-size parties.

Written Invitations

Written invitations are usually sent for large or special event parties and for formal sit-down dinner parties. They may take the form of a handwritten note, a specially printed invitation, or a commercially printed invitation.

For a handwritten note, you can use your gayest note cards. The note might read:

> Dear Sara,
> Jackie and I are planning a small cookout dinner on June 23 at 8 P.M., and we hope you'll be able to join us. There's no occasion—we just want to catch up with some friends. We do hope you can come. You can call either of us at home (387-9376) or at work (J—385-8324; me—475-8900) to let us know.
> Warm regards,
> Frank

Not too many years ago it would have been unnecessary to give such explicit directions about responding. But so many people have become seriously derelict about answering invitations that it is necessary to do so, even with the most casual invitation.

Specially printed invitations must be ordered six to eight weeks in advance of the date you plan to mail them—which means two to three months before the date of the party. They can be either informal or formal, and the stationer you order them from will help you with the wording. These invitations are especially popular for special event parties, such as a fiftieth wedding anniversary or a fortieth birthday party.

In between handwritten notes and specially printed invitations exists an array of preprinted invitations that can be purchased in any stationery store. Some are created for special occasions—birthdays and anniversaries—but there are also generic ones that you can use for any party. Blank spaces are provided for you to fill in the date and time of the party along with any other pertinent information.

YOU ARE INVITED

WHERE —
WHEN —
TIME —
WHY—

RSVP —
BY —

INFORMAL, PREPRINTED INVITATION

Please Respond

Getting people to respond to an invitation, as I mentioned earlier, is one of the harder undertakings these days. Most of us want a response whether we're planning a small dinner party or a large cocktail party. Do put this in writing—clearly. You can use the French term "RSVP," which stands for *répondez, s'il vous plaît* and translates as "Respond, please." Or you can use the more casual "Please respond."

It is very helpful to include a telephone number or address and possibly even a deadline for responding. Perhaps none of this should be necessary, but it is. It also helps to make sure the person you are inviting knows that this is a small party or a sit-down dinner.

If a party is very large, you may want to use preprinted response cards similar to the ones that are now included routinely with wedding invitations. Remember, these should be addressed and stamped.

Even with all this effort, some invitees still will not respond, and some will respond and then not attend. In the end you may just have to make an educated guess about how many guests you will have at a party.

When You Receive an Invitation

For those of you on the receiving end of an invitation, it cannot be emphasized enough how important and courteous a prompt response is. Certainly you should answer by the date requested and, if possible, within a day or two, a week at most, of receiving the invitation.

Furthermore, once you accept an invitation, there is very little reason—short of illness, death, or some major disaster—for not attending. If you're ambivalent or don't want to attend, decline the invitation. But never accept an invitation and then cavalierly brush it off.

Asking Too Early/Asking Too Late

The timing of invitations is important. An invitation for a large, somewhat formal party should go out four weeks in advance; less formal invitations can go out three to two weeks in advance; and casual invitations extended over the phone can be made any time up to a few days before the party, although the usual amount of time is five to ten days.

Generally only very intimate friends are extended last

minute invitations. But even with one's nearest and dearest—or perhaps especially with these people—it should be made clear that this is a last minute gathering so as to avoid hurt feelings.

There is a trend toward extending invitations eight and even ten weeks in advance. Unless your friends lead a very busy social life, this is extreme and too high pressured. Friends may well want to attend your annual cookout on the Fourth of July, but they may not feel like accepting an invitation to it in April. In fact, these invitations are often put aside—only to be forgotten. The smart host or hostess times invitations so they arrive neither too early nor too late.

KINDS OF PARTIES

There are many different kinds of parties, with different menus, beverages, and (most important) times. The food and beverages you serve are determined by the time of the party, and the hour on the invitation also signals your guests about what to expect, as well as what to wear.

Levels of Formality

Depending upon the host's style and preferences, parties vary in their degree of formality. A buffet dinner, for example, can be formal or informal, depending upon the service and the type of food. Simple food served on everyday dishes, where guests are expected to help themselves, is far more casual than a buffet dinner with an elegant menu, where guests are served by professional waiters and eat on good china, silver, and crystal.

The Paper vs. Glass Controversy

Formality is signaled in large part by the kinds of dishes, glasses, and flatware you use. Today, people who entertain large groups must confront the paper controversy. Increasingly, hosts are relying on paper and plastic—for napkins, dishes, glasses, and flatware. Paper napkins do make sense at a large cocktail or buffet dinner party. But there is another solution to the problem of feeding large groups, one that is far more gracious than resorting to paper or plastic.

If you plan to serve large numbers with any regularity, consider investing in inexpensive wineglasses and a set of "party" dishes made of nonbreakable (or nearly nonbreakable) glass. Very inexpensive sets of glasses and dishes can be purchased at major department stores and discount outlets.

Alternately, consider renting what you need. Dishes, glassware, flatware—indeed, anything you need can be rented. This has one additional advantage, in that you can pack up the rented items at the end of the party and send them all back—unwashed.

There are other reasons not to use paper and plastic. Food and wine do not taste particularly good from plastic and/or paper. In addition, paper plates can be hard to handle when standing and very hard to cut on. Plastic utensils pose an even greater problem, as anyone who has ever tried to cut (or, for that matter, eat) with them can attest to.

The Time of an Invitation

The hour a party is called for is an important signal regarding what to expect. Cocktail parties, for example, are always held in the early evening, because dinner will not be served. Similarly, an invitation for tea in the afternoon signals a very light meal. And an invitation for coffee and dessert, even if set for 8:00 or 8:30 P.M., indicates that there will be no meal.

A general invitation issued for 7 P.M. or after, though, implies that dinner will be served.

Apart from these generalities, here is some advice on planning specific kinds of parties:

Coffee and Dessert

Most of the time and everywhere in the country, this is a very casual party. You invite people over after dinner for coffee and dessert. The occasion may be serious, to meet a politician or new clergyperson, for example, or it may be purely social. This is an excellent and time-honored way to become better acquainted with new neighbors. It is also a good way to entertain on a work night when you don't have the time and energy for anything full scale. Book clubs, for example, often serve dessert and coffee, as do other groups that meet in the evening.

Unless the gathering is large and geared to a specific purpose, invitations for coffee or dessert are usually extended in person or by telephone. It's acceptable to ask people to come as early as 7:30 or 8:00, even though they may have to push up their dinner hour to do so. A coffee usually lasts only one or two hours. In fact, if you are sponsoring one for a politician (these are popular around the country) or for any other public cause, your invitations may specify an ending time as well as a beginning. (Such "official" events as these invariably require a written invitation.)

At a coffee, the centerpiece, of course, is freshly brewed caffeinated and decaffeinated coffee. You should also offer an assortment of teas, both caffeinated and herbal, and soft drinks. If the gathering is small, you may serve one spectacular (or at least very good) dessert. For larger parties, most hosts have a dessert table, with a variety of sweet dishes and often a fruit bowl. Two or three sweets should suffice for a group of up to twenty people, with adjustments made accordingly as the numbers go up. Another way to gauge how much to serve is to count servings. Allow one per person, and count on seconds for about 25 percent of the guests. This is probably an overestimate, but at least you will be comfortably prepared.

For a small gathering, use your nicest dessert plates and coffee cups or mugs, flatware, and linens. Don't forget to sprinkle coasters around the room if you need them. Even though this is a small party, it's fun to make it an occasion. If you're serving a larger group, you may use more casual dishes and glasses.

Service for a coffee is very simple. You can serve out of the kitchen, on a buffet table, or even at your coffee table. Except for a buffet, where guests are expected to help themselves, you should serve the dessert and coffee individually.

Coffee is accompanied by sugar and cream, although in these calorie-conscious days many hostesses also offer (or even substitute) whole or low-fat milk instead of cream. If you do serve low-fat alternatives, you might want to mention this to your guests. An elegant touch is to serve brown sugar cubes instead of refined white sugar. In any event, even though I pour the coffee, I find that my guests prefer to add their own extras.

Espresso is popular now and many people like to serve it after dinner, not least because it offers a proportionately smaller dose of caffeine, one that shouldn't keep anyone up late. If you are planning to serve espresso, then by all means brew your own. And never, as one friend of mine did, buy an espresso maker and then plan to use it the same night for company. A little practice is required to master these somewhat complex machines, and it's better to do this before you invite others over to indulge in this passion.

Espresso is traditionally served in small cups and saucers,

accompanied by small spoons. Condiments include sugar and small pieces of lemon peel. Cream or milk is never served with espresso. There are perfectly acceptable brewed decaffeinated espressos, which your guests may appreciate being offered.

Tea

Does an invitation to tea sound like something from a bygone era? Well, tea is making a comeback, and many people applaud its renewed popularity because it is such a civilized way to entertain.

While coffee and dessert are served after dinner, tea is an afternoon ritual—a sort of pick-me-up for the late afternoon period. As a rule, tea is served between 4 and 6 P.M., although the hours can be—and often are—stretched at either end.

Even more than an invitation to coffee, an invitation to tea—which may be extended by phone or note—calls for your nicest dishes and flatware and your prettiest napkins. The tea should be specially brewed, which means you should use loose-leaf tea if possible, teabags if not. Many purists object to teabags in any form, but if they are high quality, they can be as good as and occasionally better than a low-grade leaf tea.

If you are just rediscovering the pleasures of tea, you may need this refresher course on how to brew a good pot:

1. Bring a kettle of water to the boiling point.
2. Meanwhile, rinse out a teapot with hot water and dry it carefully.
3. Add the tea leaves, either in the pot or in a tea holder. Use one teaspoon of leaves or one teabag per cup.

4.   Pour boiling water over the tea.

5.   Let the tea steep for four minutes before serving.

Tea is served with lemon wedges, sugar or honey, and milk. People either take lemon or milk, not both. Cream is never used in tea. It is best to serve the milk and the lemon on the side and let your guests help themselves. Also, have some extra hot water on hand for those who prefer a weak tea; you can mix the water with the tea when you pour it.

Any good black or oolong tea is suitable for the afternoon; this includes the mild Darjeeling, the stronger smoke lapsang souchong, and the traditional Earl Grey. Herbal teas, which are (strictly speaking) not teas at all but infusions, can also be served. In fact, it is smart to serve a selection of these as well as the caffeinated teas. Mint and fruit-flavored teas are nice afternoon pick-me-ups.

As for the tea menu, bite-size sandwiches are traditional, as are small pastries and baked goods, such as scones, individual fruit tarts, and cookies. Unfrosted, not overly sweet loaf cakes (such as apple or pear), zucchini and carrot bread, or a number of variations on pound cake are all appropriate for tea. You may also serve fruit and cheese.

Cocktail Parties

Like tea, cocktail parties, which were popular in the fifties, are making a comeback. It is surprising that they were out of favor so long, since this is one of the easier ways to entertain. Cocktail parties can be as simple as having six friends over for drinks and hors d'oeuvres before another event or as involved as having sixty people for a full-blown party. They are an excellent way to pay back other invitations, especially if you have a limited budget.

Invitations

The first step to organizing a large cocktail party—drawing up the guest list—is also the easiest. Quite simply, you can include anyone and everyone. In fact, the most successful parties mix young and old as well as friends, acquaintances, and business colleagues. The more mixed the guest list is, the more interesting the party will be.

Printed invitations are good for a large party, but if you're having a few friends over for drinks, you won't want to bother and will simply call people to invite them.

Cocktail parties are held in the early evening—typically between 5 and 9 P.M.—with the idea that guests go on to dinner later. You may ask your guests to respond or not, but in either event, count on receiving regrets from about a fourth to a third of the people you invite, and overinvite accordingly.

Space

Even before you plan your guest list, you need to consider how many people you can fit into your living room or wherever else you plan to hold the party. Obviously the size of the room limits the number you can entertain, but cocktail parties hum along better when they are full of people. Another key to a successful cocktail party is to make your guests stand up—that way they'll be more likely to circulate. Here's how to plan crowd logistics:

- Remove as much furniture as you can or push it out of the way. You don't want people to have a place to sit down at a party like this.
- Remove breakables and small objects that could be knocked over.
- Make room for coats, umbrellas, briefcases, and other

similar items in a room other than where the party will be held. A bed suffices, an empty closet will do but is probably too much work, and best of all is to rent a coat rack (if you live in an apartment, you can usually position it in the hallway right outside your front door—provided you have invited your neighbors to the party).

• Make sure your bathroom is clean and well stocked for a crowd. This means several rolls of toilet paper and lots of tissue and other paper products. (Cloth towels should always be favored over paper, but it's not realistic to use real hand towels for a crowd, so buy some nice, high-quality hand paper towels.)

• Figure out in advance where you'll set up the bar—or bars. If you are entertaining fewer than fifty, one bar will suffice. More than that, and you'll need more bars. Situate the bars in out-of-the-way yet accessible places.

• Have a few tables around where guests can leave their used glasses and plates when they are finished with them.

Drinks

Because many people no longer regularly serve hard liquor, I've been asked if one can have a cocktail party and serve only wine and beer. You may of course serve anything you please at your party, but if you will be limiting the drinks in this way, then I suggest that you not bill the social occasion as a cocktail party. When people are invited for cocktails, this is basically what they expect—and what they should be served.

Your drink choices can be more limited at a small party than they can be at a large one. You can offer wine, for example, but you should be at least minimally prepared to serve other drinks as well. This means you should have on hand at least a quart each of Scotch, whiskey, vodka, and gin, plus a good assortment of mixers.

A large cocktail party should have a complete bar—hard liquor, wine, beer, soft drinks, and, these days, the ubiquitous bottled water. Here's how to calculate what you will need:

- Plan on each guest drinking two to three drinks during the course of the party. About a third of the guests will consume the third drink.

- Allow 1.5 ounces of liquor in each drink, which means you will get twenty-one drinks from a fifth (or quart) of liquor.

- For every fifty guests, you will need a half-gallon each of vodka, gin, and Scotch—the staples, so to speak. Beyond this, you will need a fifth each of the less popular liquors such as rum, bourbon, and whiskey.

- Keep in mind, though, that liquor preferences are highly dependent upon where you live and on the season. Southerners prefer bourbon, for example, while northerners lean toward Scotch. Everyone drinks more vodka and gin in the summer.

- In terms of mixers and soft drinks, for fifty people lay in the following amounts: cola and clear soft beverages, four half-gallons each kind; diet soda, two half-gallons; and bottled water, five gallons.

All these quantities are more than you will need, but cocktail party guests are notoriously unpredictable, and you won't want to run out of anything. These quantities can be scaled up or down depending upon the size of the guest list.

Here's how to calculate the wine for a cocktail party:

- Allow six glasses per bottle. (It's smart to use smaller wineglasses at a cocktail party rather than the currently fashionable four- to five-ounce size.) Try for wineglasses that hold about two and a half ounces per serving.

- Buy a third more white than red.
- Especially in large urban areas, overstock on wine, since this has become the preferred drink, even at cocktail parties.
- For fifty guests plan on fifteen to twenty bottles, two-thirds white, one-third red.

Cocktail Party Food

As a rule, finger foods (preferably ones that can be eaten standing up) are preferred at cocktail parties. Hors d'oeuvres and canapés—appealing, bite-size morsels—were invented to go with cocktails. Other typical cocktail party fare includes a cheese board, cheese sticks, bread sticks, nuts, olives, small pizzas and/or hot dogs, kebabs (chicken, beef, and pork), and vegetable hors d'oeuvres. Crudités are always welcome in these diet-conscious times. For something more elegant (and expensive), you might serve bite-size sandwiches, as well as shrimp, oysters, and other seafood.

When planning a cocktail menu, remember that your guests are supposed to go on to dinner elsewhere. This doesn't mean the menu should be skimpy, only that you need not worry about a main course.

A Word about Help

If all this sounds like a bit of work, it is. In fact, a cocktail party (or, for that matter, any party) usually benefits from some outside help. Anytime you are serving more than thirty or so guests, plan to hire bartenders and possibly food servers as well.

You should also plan to separate the food and beverage service. Both can be served from central places—a bar, a food table—or you can hire bartenders to take people's drink orders and servers to pass platters of food, but the food and drink should come from two different places if at all possible. If space is tight, serve food out of the kitchen and set up a bar in another room.

Buffet Dinner

A buffet dinner is an excellent way to entertain a large or small group of friends. The emphasis here, unlike at a cocktail party, is on the food, and on this occasion you do try to arrange for your guests to sit down at least while they eat. You need not provide seating for every single guest, though, which means you should plan food that people can eat either standing up or from a plate perched on their laps. Guests are expected to serve themselves from the buffet table, or they may be served, more formally, by servers who stand behind the table.

Invitations

If you are inviting many people, use written invitations and include a request for a response since you are serving a full meal. When entertaining a few friends, you can telephone the invitation. Depending upon personal inclination and local customs, dinner parties usually start around 7 P.M., although they may begin as late as 9 P.M. When children are included, many hosts start the party even earlier, around 6 P.M.

The Menu

Easy-to-eat fork foods are the key to a successful buffet dinner. Stews, curries, and creoles work especially well. Roasts are popular because they are easy to prepare, but they are much harder to eat since they have to be cut. If you want to serve roasted meat, think about sandwiches.

As a side dish, rice is easier to eat than potatoes, unless the potatoes have been cooked in bite-size pieces. Other acceptable side dishes include vegetables and condiments, bread, and salads. Dessert can be almost anything that can be eaten with just a fork, or you can stick to finger foods such as cookies, brownies, and fruit. To complete the meal, serve coffee and tea.

Strive for balance and variety in the buffet menu, particularly if you are serving many different people with myriad tastes. Hosts today usually plan some dishes for meat lovers and some for vegetarians. Apart from this, you can mix hot and cold foods. For a group of twenty or fewer people, you can serve one or two main dishes and side dishes in each category. As the guest list expands, the amount of food should expand accordingly.

Drinks

Drinks at a buffet dinner are much simpler than those at a cocktail party. If you like, you can limit them to wine that complements the food. Fill in with beer, if it suits your menu, and soft drinks for those who don't drink alcohol.

Logistics

Depending upon the number of guests, food is served from one or more buffet tables, and guests either help themselves or are served by waiters behind the tables. It is a good idea to set up the bar, however simple, elsewhere. When planning the buffet table, think about how guests can most conveniently work their way around as they fill their plates. A condiment for meat should be placed nearby, so that guests can see and take some as they are selecting their meat. A sample buffet table is shown opposite.

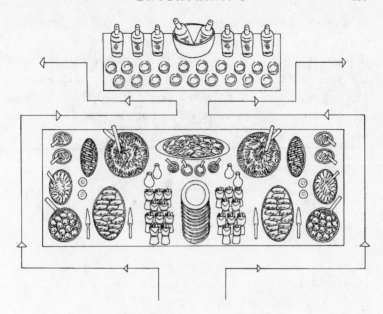

BUFFET TABLE

A Word about Help

Anytime you are feeding more than twenty or twenty-five people at a dinner of this sort, you'll probably need extra hands to help. A bartender relieves some of the pressure, and servers may be used to replenish the table, clear between courses, and handle the cleanup.

Sit-down Dinner

The most elaborate and formal kind of party you can give is a sit-down dinner, although some sit-down dinners are quite casual.

Choosing the Guest List

The guest list for this kind of party needs to be well thought out. You will want your guests to be compatible with one another—guests who aren't can lead to a deadly dull evening. This doesn't preclude trying for a bit of balance, though, by inviting guests of different professions, interests, and ages. In fact, this can make for a lively evening. Fortunately the days are over when a host worried about having an even number of men and women at the table or an even number of diners.

Invitations

Invitations to a formal dinner party are usually telephoned. But if this is a special occasion, mailed invitations might be in order—either commercially printed fill-in invitations or ones that you have printed especially for the occasion. Alternately, you could send handwritten notes. A response is obviously necessary for this kind of party, and it's not usual to give people a deadline for responding.

Sit-down dinner parties begin anywhere from 7 to 9 P.M., with 8 P.M. being the most traditional hour. If you are giving a sit-down lunch, the usual time is anywhere from noon to 1 P.M., depending upon local custom.

The Menu

The sky's the limit when planning an intimate dinner party, but most hosts take account of the time and energy involved in preparing the meal (especially if they are doing the cooking themselves), as well as the expense. Savvy hosts know that they can feed a group inexpensively and quite well simply by selecting the menu wisely. A good dinner party menu balances light and heavy dishes, colors, and types of food.

It is possible (but hard work!) for one or two people to prepare and serve up to eight to ten guests at a sit-down dinner without any outside help. The ideal number, however, is probably six. If you are inviting more than eight to ten, you will need help, if only to serve the food while it's hot. Help can take the shape of a caterer or food servers, although the two often go hand in hand.

These days it is rare at even the most formal dinner to be served more than four or five courses, and many excellent meals are simpler still. Nevertheless, it is useful to understand the distinctions among all five courses:

First course: Appetizers. These may be served with drinks in the living room. Choices may be as simple as nuts or olives or as complicated as canapés.

Second course: Soup, vegetable, or fish. This is a light course, served in small portions.

Third course: Entrée. This, the main course, should complement the first course. For example, if you served smoked salmon, you would probably opt for a meat entrée or a dish that is completely different. The main course could be a one-dish meal such as stew or it could be a roast or fish with vegetables and a starch.

Fourth course: Salad. This is the palate cleanser, which is why it works better served after the entrée. The traditional French salad consists of greens in a vinaigrette, but Americans tend to like a fuller salad, with tomatoes and other vegetables. Keep in mind, though, that at a dinner party the salad will follow several other courses, so diners won't need or want much. Alternatively, you could serve this course after the appetizers and before the entrée.

Fifth course: Dessert and coffee. These days many health-conscious hosts also serve fruit, which, when served with cheese, can be either a substitute or an addition to dessert.

You can choose to serve all these courses or a selection of them. I have been to wonderful dinner parties where the entire meal was a hearty stew served with a crusty French bread and a salad.

Logistics

Guests should arrive pretty much at the designated hour.
You should greet each one personally, take his or her coat,
make introductions to others who have arrived, and offer a
drink and a place to sit within the group.

A smart host doesn't prolong the cocktail hour; dinner is
best served thirty minutes or so after the guests arrive. You
simply announce that it is ready and lead your guests to the
dinner table.

Of course, the table should be set as beautifully as possible. For a formal dinner party, this means your best dishes,
flatware, and glassware, plus candles and often a centerpiece
as well. But even for a casual dinner, there are many opportunities for creativity, both in the dishes you choose to use
and in the way you set up the table.

The standard centerpiece is a bouquet of flowers, which
should not be so high as to interfere with your guests' conversations with one another. But I've seen fruits and vegetables and even, on one occasion, some beautiful rocks make
stunning centerpieces. You are limited only by your imagi-
nation.

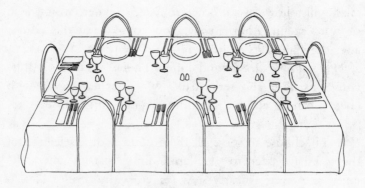

TABLE SET FOR A DINNER PARTY

Seating is usually assigned by the hostess, either via place cards at each setting or more informally by telling people where you would like them to sit. If there are to be more than eight people at the table, put some thought into the seating arrangements, since people will break up into small groups to talk over dinner. With luck and a little planning, those you seat next to one another should have enough in common to carry on an amiable conversation. At best there could be a real connection between the guests seated next to each other, although you might have to draw it out during dinner. If you are entertaining fewer than six guests, the table will probably talk as a group, and you need not worry very much about people's affinities for one another.

Rules also govern seating honored guests such as the person whose birthday you are celebrating, an old friend who is visiting, or a dignitary, such as a clergyperson. A female guest of honor sits at the host's right and a male guest of honor at the hostess's left. A single person entertaining puts the guest of honor, if there is one, at his right. A second guest of honor goes to the left. The host and hostess usually occupy the end seats at the table.

There are at least three ways to serve food at a sit-down dinner. In family-style service, platters and serving bowls are passed among the guests, who help themselves. Plates may also be brought in from the kitchen with the food already on them. Finally, servers—either the hosts or hired help—can enter with platters of food and carry them around to individual diners. Guests can either help themselves or servers can wait upon each diner, although this latter method requires at least two servers. Regardless of whether food is brought in on plates or platters, it is usually served from the left, which makes it easier for a right-handed world. Used plates are removed on the right.

At a sit-down dinner, each course is cleared before the

next one is brought out, but no plates should be cleared until everyone has finished dining. Servers should take plates away individually; never should they be stacked up unceremoniously at the table.

When diners sit down, the second (or first) course is usually on the table. Bread, salt and pepper, and condiments should also be conveniently situated on the table. Food can be carved at the table or in the kitchen, whichever is easier.

Beverages

Several beverages are served at a sit-down dinner. Sherry is the traditional drink with soup, and white and red wine are served with the first course and entrée. Wine is not served— or drunk—with salad because it fights with the vinegar in the dressing. An after-dinner liqueur may be offered with— or after—dessert and coffee, although many hosts today skip this. Most diners also enjoy a glass of water, although this is not necessary and its presence on the table may vary with local custom.

Wine should always be chosen for its affinity to the food that is being served. The much touted rule is that red wines go with red meat and white wines go with fish, but true oenophiles know that this rule is meant to be broken. A heavy poultry dish such as coq au vin, for example, is not only made with red wine but is meant to be accompanied by it as well. Turkey fares at least as well with a red wine as with a white. Even certain fish cooked in certain ways cries out for a red rather than a white wine.

A better rule of thumb is to match heavy, substantial dishes with heavier, bolder wines, white or red, while serving lighter dishes with lighter wines (which usually, but not always, translates as a white). Sweet wines go with dessert and are never appropriately served with other foods.

Champagne is versatile and goes with appetizers, some

main dishes (turkey, for example), and dessert. Its only barrier is its expense. A good French champagne—and only the French make real champagne—will cost quite a bit. You may find that other sparkling wines (from California, for example) are just as festive as champagne, but less expensive.

Except for the after-dinner glasses, all glasses for the beverage service should be on the table when diners sit down. As each wine course is finished, its glass is removed.

Now having said all this, I must acknowledge that wine service has gotten very simple these days. Many sophisticated hosts and hostesses serve only one wine with dinner, and many now offer guests a choice of either white or red, regardless of the food being served. If you are unsure how to select wines, you can always throw yourself on the mercy of a good wine merchant, who will be happy to help you with selections that match your menu.

Leaving the Table

The hostess or host decides when it is time to leave the table. Some like to serve dessert and coffee at the table, while others prefer to do this in the living room. If the meal has been lengthy, it is a nice change of pace to move to another room, if possible. To adjourn the table, simply say, "Let's have dessert in the living room."

When the Party Is Over

A really good dinner party combines great food, wonderful drinks, and fascinating people and as such can go on for hours. A dinner party that lasts until the wee hours of the morning may not please the host as much as one might imagine, since he has probably spent the entire day cooking in the kitchen and the day before that shopping. As a general rule, guests linger about an hour after the dinner before leaving. If you must leave earlier or are the first to do so, try to make a quick exit so you don't break up the party.

OTHER PARTIES

Below is a roundup of some other types of parties, with suggestions to help make each a success.

Brunch and Lunch

These are smaller, lighter versions of a dinner party. At a brunch, the emphasis is on breakfast foods, while a lunch calls for lighter and fewer courses of a dinner party type. Menu planning and logistics are the same as for dinner. A lunch can be formal or informal; if it is formal, the table is set with flowers and candles, although the latter should never be lighted during the day.

Guests usually arrive promptly for a lunch and don't linger, especially if they must go back to work or have a late afternoon engagement. Brunch, a far more leisurely meal, is usually held on the weekend and can begin anywhere from eleven to one, depending upon local dining customs.

Potluck Dinner

This is a special dinner party where everyone contributes something—usually a dish or a course. Potlucks are a favorite of churches and other organizations and groups. There is only one secret to a potluck, and that is to coordinate the menu so there is some balance in the meal. One person should be in charge of doing this. The host or hostess (the one whose home is used) generally provides dishes, flatware, glasses, and table linens.

Cookout/Barbecue

This favorite way of summer entertaining is popular all over the country. It is a simple meal, because the main course is usually cooked outside on a grill. The only tricky thing about a cookout is the unpredictability of the weather. A hostess can either list a rain date (difficult since the food must be purchased) or be prepared to move the party inside if the weather is inclement. At the most elegant outdoor meals, real plates and flatware are used rather than plastic, but this is one occasion when paper and plastic are acceptable. Cookouts and barbecues are often planned around a theme: the Fourth of July, a Hawaiian luau, a garden party, Bastille Day—any occasion can be an excuse for this kind of informal party.

Open House

This is a time-honored way to entertain large groups. Open houses are especially popular around the holidays and in some parts of the country as housewarmings. An open house is a cross between a cocktail party and a buffet dinner. The menu can be as simple as punch and dessert, or, as more often is the case, a meal is served.

You can telephone invitations, but written invitations also work well since this is usually a large party. It's reasonable to ask people to respond since you'll want an idea of how many will be attending. Open houses usually last at least four hours, sometimes six, and guests may come any time during those hours. (Only the most boorish guest would plant himself on your doorstep when the party begins and stay until it ends.)

To accommodate the crowd, the hours for an open house

are often staggered; that is, some guests are invited to come between 2 and 4 P.M., while a second group is invited to come between 3 and 6 P.M. To avoid a lull, there is usually some overlap between the two.

SPECIAL OCCASION PARTIES

Special occasion parties include showers, anniversaries, and birthday parties.

Showers

A shower is given to honor a friend who is getting married or is expecting or has had a baby. It should be given by friends, never by family members. Only close friends and family are invited, and everyone who is invited to a bridal shower must also be invited to the wedding.

It is almost never a good idea to plan a surprise shower for anyone, either a bride or a pregnant woman. Some people simply do not want a bridal shower. And some groups customarily do not give a baby shower until after the birth. Many Jewish expectant parents, for example, do not even bring baby furniture home until after the child has been born.

Showers used to be women-only parties, but many showers today are coeducational. A wedding shower, in particular, may have a theme such as appliances, wine, lingerie, kitchen and bath, and so on. Guests are expected to bring a gift related to the theme.

A shower can be brunch, lunch, or dinner, or much lighter refreshments. A specially decorated cake is usually served as dessert. Written invitations are generally sent, and responses are expected.

Anniversary Parties

Anniversary parties are most often given for silver and golden anniversaries, but any one in between may be celebrated with a party. Children may give such a party for their parents.

Anniversary celebrations can be formal or informal. Either way, written invitations are usually sent, and responses are expected. Especially elegant for an affair of this kind is the dinner dance, which is exactly what it sounds like: dinner with dancing afterward. These are often dressy events. If people have traveled to attend the party, a full dinner should be served. A specially decorated cake, served with champagne, usually caps off the evening.

Gifts are often discouraged, but guests may bring them if they choose. Close family members and friends will probably want to give a present in any event.

Birthday Parties for Adults

Birthday parties run the gamut from small and casual to large and formal. They are given by family or friends. A person can even have a party for herself—provided she picks up the tab and as long as gifts are discouraged.

Usually adults have birthday parties to mark a significant age, like the turn of a decade. Special celebrations are also often held at "crossroads" birthdays, which in our culture are eighteen, twenty-one, sixty-five, and seventy-five.

An adult birthday party can be anything from the most elaborate and formal dinner dance to a casual, jokey bash. Once a person has reached a certain age, nostalgia provides good party themes. One hostess celebrated her fortieth birthday with a fifties party and spent the weeks before it searching for just the right outfit to wear, right down to the poodle felt skirt and sunglasses. She had a friend drive a 1955 Cadillac convertible (oh, those fins!) onto her lawn and hired a photographer to take pictures of guests in it.

Birthday Parties for Children

Although there is a trend toward elaborate parties for children, these are usually wasted on very young children, and they seem a bit extravagant to have every year. When the child is between one and three, birthday celebrations are best kept simple, with the guest list limited to family members and very close friends. The child is too young to know what the party is all about, so the celebration is really for the adults anyway. A decorated cake is usually served. Invitations, like the party, are informally telephoned.

By the time a child reaches three to four years of age, he may be ready for a birthday party with his peers. Children's birthday parties are generally held in the afternoon, and last $1\frac{1}{2}$ to 2 hours. These are usually highly ritualized events. Games or other kinds of entertainment are scheduled, lunch is served, gifts are opened, and if all goes well, the little guys leave before naptime and crankiness sets in.

Paper and plastic are not only acceptable, but recommended. In keeping with children's tastes, the food should be simple as well: hamburgers and hot dogs are proven crowd pleasers, and ice cream and cake are the time-honored desserts. Simple favors (and, in some parts of the country, very fancy and expensive favors) are usually given to guests at young children's parties.

By the time a child is in her teens, she is old enough to participate in planning her own party and will want to invite her friends—perhaps at the exclusion of her relatives. (Lots of parents schedule a peer party and a second, smaller gathering for the family.)

The big question that arises when planning the guest list for an older child's birthday party is whether or not the entire school class must be invited. If possible, and the class is not too large, this is the most tactful thing to do. Even if a smaller party is in order for some reason, it's still a nice touch to arrange for a celebration at school, if permitted, that includes everyone. In some schools this is customary; in others, not. A school celebration can be as simple as taking cake or cupcakes to school—enough for everyone, of course.

If your child is having a smaller party that will exclude some classmates, then this is as good a time as any to teach him discretion. A wise parent gently explores to see whether anyone is being excluded because of a grudge, a handicap, cliquishness, or some other less than kind reason. You do your child a favor to teach him inclusiveness, and birthday parties offer an excellent opportunity to do this. Sit down with your child and discuss how the excluded child might feel, as well as a few justifiable reasons for excluding someone (he's really not a friend) as opposed to bad ones (he doesn't have nice clothes). You can also teach your child that it will be kinder not to mention the party to those who are not invited.

Fortunately parties get easier to organize as children get older, not least because older children often prefer an event-oriented celebration, and those usually happen somewhere other than in your house.

Surprise Parties

Some people like to be surprised; others abhor it. Each of us should know—and honor—our partner's or friend's preferences. If someone tells you he does not want a surprise party, then the key to a successful party is to believe him and not plan one.

If you do feel that a surprise is appropriate and acceptable to the guest of honor, then there is still one important rule: Give the honoree the chance to look at least as good as the guests. Don't surprise someone who is still in bed, or hopping out of the shower, or just finishing a grueling afternoon of raking leaves and wants nothing more than a hot shower and a long nap. Plan the party for an appropriate time, and somehow (subterfuge is permissible here) make sure that the guest of honor is as well dressed as the guests.

COMMON ENTERTAINING PROBLEMS

Some problems are so common that every host or hostess runs into them sooner or later. Even so, they often leave us unsure what to do—or less than eager to do it. Here are some guidelines for those inevitable awkward moments connected to entertaining.

Extra Guests

If you are invited to a party and find yourself with an extra person, your guest, on your hands, you can call your host and mention that you can't come because you have a houseguest. It is then up to the host to decide whether or not to extend the invitation to your guest. If the host does not or (as is more likely the case) cannot, then you have two choices: Go without your guest or stay home. If your guest is an unexpected one, it is entirely appropriate to say that you have a party to attend and then leave the guest at home for a few hours.

At a small party or a sit-down dinner, the host should not

even be burdened with the knowledge that you have a houseguest. And it's rude to drop out at the last minute, since your host or hostess may well be counting on you to complete the table. Surprise guest or not, you are expected to show up as if nothing had happened.

Smoking, Drugs, and Drinking

More and more of us are going smokeless these days—and we usually extend the ban to our guests. If you are a visitor in someone's home, note that the absence of ashtrays can almost always be taken as a sign that smoking is not welcomed.

Some guests make provisions for smokers (the back hall or the back porch), while others do not or cannot. Either way you must abide by the rules, especially since some smoking bans are prompted by allergies. Never go into a room in someone's house to smoke unless you know that your host won't mind.

Drugs are less of a problem these days than they were a few years ago. A host or hostess has every right not to expect any illegal drug use from a guest, and you should comply with this. If you use drugs at a friend's house, you put both yourself *and* your friend at risk. Such behavior is not only rude, but downright hostile.

Drinking poses another kind of problem: it is legal, and it is difficult for one adult to tell another not to imbibe. Still, no one appreciates a sloppy drunk; embarrass yourself and others a few times this way and you'll no doubt find yourself being dropped from several guest lists.

Basically it is up to each individual to keep his drinking under control. If an adult does not do this, and begins to spoil the party or harass others, then the host may have to take some action. When someone has become offensive at a party because of drinking or another reason, it is your right—and some would say duty—as host to help that person leave the party, even at an early hour. Ask someone to take the offender home, or better yet, call a cab or car service.

Hosts are no longer obliged to humor a drunken guest, serve him coffee (which doesn't sober anyone up anyway), or otherwise cater to him. Simply send him home. And if he ever wants to be invited again, he'd better come up with a monster-size apology the next day.

The Good Host

As host, it is your job to make sure everyone who comes to your home feels welcome. Here's how to do this:

- Greet all arrivals personally and warmly.
- Introduce guests to other guests and try to settle them into a group or conversation.
- Put together people whom you have reason to believe have something in common. You cannot control the flow every minute, but you can help it along initially and at certain points.
- Rescue wallflowers. It is your job to talk to shy people and do what you can to bring them out. At a large party this means keeping an eye out for the person who is withdrawing; at a smaller party it means bringing everyone into the conversation.
- Never argue with or insult a guest in your home, nor should you permit one guest to do this to another. In other words, everyone is expected to be on best behavior. If you invited your new neighbors to a Fourth of July barbecue only to discover that their politics are in the opposite direc-

tion from yours, you must still be gracious and friendly—even if they will never darken your doorstep again.

• Keep the food and beverages flowing. A generous table is the easiest way to gain a reputation as a loving host or hostess. Always buy more than you think you'll need, and make sure it is available to your guests.

• Party within your means. No one is comfortable—or impressed—at a party where the host has clearly blown his last $100 on caviar. It's an awkward situation, to say the least.

• The corollary to this is, buy the very best of what you *can* afford. If you can afford only beer, then serve a really good or interesting beer. If you cannot afford shrimp, then settle on the less expensive turkey and buy the best of that.

• Laugh at disaster when it strikes. Wineglasses get broken, rugs get stained, chairs get broken—this is the price of entertaining. Always, always be gracious when something happens. Reassure your guest that the wineglasses were cheap, that the rug is old, and the chair has no sentimental value.

• Finally, never, never let a guest depart drunk if he is driving. Arrange for someone to take him home, or call a car for him.

THE GOOD GUEST

Good guests are in demand, especially these days when they seem to be a vanishing species. If you enjoy being entertained and want to be everybody's favorite guest, here are a few simple rules to follow:

• Respond to all invitations promptly.
• Once you have accepted an invitation, never cancel except for an emergency or illness.
• On the other hand, don't go places when you are ill.

No one likes to have a guest walk in with the flu or even a cold and then give it to everyone else.

• Arrive on time. Do, however, pay attention to local custom on this point. In large cities like New York, Los Angeles, and Chicago, for example, parties typically begin an hour or more after the time on the invitation. In other parts of the country, you would miss the food if you came that late. Almost everywhere, you should arrive on time for a dinner invitation, since some foods are spoiled if they cook too long.

• Don't arrive early. Don't show up even five minutes early, as your hostess may not be ready for you.

• Don't be the last to depart—at least not on a regular basis.

• Be a good mixer. Introduce yourself to others. Any time you are a guest in someone's home, it is expected that you will talk with the other guests.

• Dress appropriately. Wear casual clothes to casual parties and dressy clothes to dressy parties. If you aren't sure what to wear, ask your host. If you do wear the wrong thing, ignore the faux pas and have a good time anyway. For all anyone knows, you're headed to another party, where black tie is requested.

• Never switch place cards. It's the hostess's prerogative to seat her guests in any manner she chooses and your duty not to murmur a word in protest.

• Never insult another guest or deliberately pick a fight with one.

• Offer to help. And when the offer is declined, as it probably will be, don't force your way in. Sit down, relax, and let the host do the work.

• Say good-bye to your host when you leave and tell him what a wonderful time you have had—even if you haven't.

- Call your hostess within a few days of a party or send a note letting her know again what a wonderful time you had.

WHEN BAD THINGS (LIKE BREAKAGE) HAPPEN TO GOOD PEOPLE

Even the best-intentioned guest occasionally spills or breaks something in someone else's house. When this happens to you, always level with your host about what has happened. Never, ever try to cover up, and don't do anything to clean up or fix it yourself unless your host asks you to. You may think soda water is great for taking up a red wine stain on white carpet, but your host may have a better idea—and it *is* his carpet.

If whatever you damaged can be repaired or replaced, or if it is at all valuable, it is up to you to repair or replace it despite your host's protests. Put another way, it is your host's job to protest that you need not do anything, and it is your job to replace or fix whatever you broke. There are a couple of exceptions. If you break a cheap wineglass, you need not worry about replacing it, but if the wineglass is crystal, you should send a replacement right away.

If the object cannot be repaired or replaced, and it is valuable, then you owe your host a very nice present, although it need not be a duplicate of what you broke. And whether you break something small or large, another follow-up apology the next day is a nice touch. Even nicer, depending upon how much damage you did, is a bouquet of flowers.

AS YOU ENTERTAIN, YOU WILL DISCOVER FOR YOURSELF the pleasure of giving parties, and you will also develop your own style of entertaining. There are great pleasures to be derived from planning a special occasion for friends and then watching it come off well. Best of all, the more you entertain, the better you become at it.

Chapter 7

TABLE MANNERS

✳

IN THESE DAYS OF CASUAL EATING AND CARRY-OUT FOOD, it's hard to imagine that table manners still matter, but they do. Right or wrong, people still judge others by their table manners. And many a person has lost a job—and a friend—because his were not up to snuff.

Fortunately table manners are much less fussy now than they were a few decades ago. As meals have gotten simpler, so have table manners. Gone are the eight-course meals, replaced by healthier three- or four-course repasts and a new easiness about dining. Even with the new informality, though, it's helpful to know your way around a table.

Table manners are like a road map: they can guide you through the toughest meal, when you're confronted with a food you've never seen, for example, or a glass whose use you can't begin to divine.

THE PLACE SETTING

A place setting is what you encounter when you sit down to dinner either at home or in a restaurant. It can be informal or formal.

The more formal the place setting, the more flatware (and, for that matter, glasses and plates) you will see when you sit down. A formal place setting is designed to accommodate a meal of four or five courses, while fewer courses—usually one to three—are the rule at an informal dinner.

The illustration below shows a place setting for a formal meal consisting of five courses: an appetizer, a soup, an entrée, a salad, and dessert and coffee (which are usually, but not always, served together these days).

The small seafood fork on the right resting against the soup spoon is used to eat a first course of seafood—seafood cocktail, oysters, clams, shrimp, and other similar foods. It

FORMAL PLACE SETTING

may be placed against the outside spoon, as illustrated, or to the left with the forks.

When another food is served as the first course, you will use the fork on the outside left of the place setting. This versatile piece of flatware is larger than a seafood fork but smaller than the place fork and is used to eat fish or another first course. (A true fish fork has a left outermost tine specially shaped to "pick" at the fish for bones, but many silversmiths no longer craft forks with this distinction.) If needed, use the place knife (the large one on the right) to eat the first course, unless a fish knife (small and pointed) has been provided, as it sometimes is with a first course of fish.

The second course, which is soup, is eaten with the large spoon to the right of the knife.

The next course is often salad, which is eaten with the middle fork. Alternately, the salad course may be served after the entrée. When this happens, the salad fork is placed next to the plate, and the entrée fork is placed in the middle.

However, in the illustration at left, the entrée comes after the salad and it is eaten with the large place fork and the place knife.

The dessert fork and spoon go above the plate, or they may be brought in with the dessert. A good way to remember the placement of these utensils is to think of them as growing out of their similar utensils. For example, the dessert fork's tines face away from the other forks, not into them.

The dessert spoon often doubles as the coffee spoon, or another spoon may be brought in to serve coffee. On some occasions you may find the coffee spoon between the soup spoon and the knife.

Finally, the formal place setting contains a small knife used for buttering bread and rolls. This rests across the butter plate, which goes slightly to the left and above the dinner plate.

If all this seems complicated, keep in mind that even at a formal dinner, you should not encounter more than three spoons—or forks or knives—at your place setting. Additional flatware is brought to the table as needed. Although four forks are shown on page 176, this is for illustration only; you would not usually be served a seafood cocktail and a fish course at the same meal.

Now let's walk through the flatware for an informal meal, which is shown at right. This place setting is intended to serve three courses: salad, entrée, and dessert and coffee.

Since the salad is the first course at this meal, the salad fork is on the far left. If it were served after the entrée, the fork would be placed to the right of the place fork. If a knife is needed to cut your salad, use the place knife. When you're finished, unless you are asked to keep your knife, put it on the salad plate, and your host or the waiter will bring you another knife.

The place fork and place knife are used to eat the entrée.

The dessert fork is brought in with the dessert. Alternately, it could be placed above the plate along with the dessert/coffee spoon. In this illustration, the spoon to the right of the knife is the coffee/dessert spoon.

The Golden Rule of Utensil Use

Let's say, worst-case scenario, that you're at your boss's house for dinner and everything you've read about which fork to use escapes you. Facing you are three forks and two spoons, and you haven't the faintest notion which one to pick up first. Don't worry, there's a "golden rule" of utensils that will help you get through this trying situation.

It's very simple: Always work your way from the outside

INFORMAL PLACE SETTING

to the inside. This means starting with the outermost fork or spoon and moving in toward your plate. This rule is virtually foolproof, provided the host has set the table correctly. If he hasn't, it's not your fault if you use the wrong utensil.

Glassware

As for glassware, the illustration on page 176 shows the water glass, red-wine glass, and white-wine glass that are typical at a formal dinner. The illustration above shows the single wineglass and water glass that are more usual at an informal dinner. Glasses are arranged at the upper right of the place setting. The water glass is usually positioned at the tip of the knife, and the others are placed around it.

Which Glass Is Right?

Deciding which glass to use is usually easy, because glasses are filled automatically by your host as various courses are served. In addition, at most informal meals only one wine is served, so there is only one wineglass to contend with.

Other glasses you might encounter, depending upon the formality of the meal:

Sherry Glass

This looks like a miniature wineglass. Sherry is served with soup or occasionally with an appetizer. Sherry glasses or other similar small glasses are also used to serve after-dinner sweet wines or liqueurs.

The Generic Wineglass •

It's popular to use the same shape wineglass for both red and white wine, although oenophiles still prefer to use specially shaped glasses for various wines, on the grounds that glass shapes enhance the flavor of the wine.

Sherry   Wine   Cognac   Champagne

GLASSES

Cognac Glass

This glass is designed to hold cognac but can also be used for other after-dinner drinks such as whiskey or brandy. The round bowl of the glass is meant to be cupped in the hands in order to warm the liquor slightly.

Champagne Glass

These are either flute shaped, tulip shaped, or flat. Champagne is most often served with appetizers and with dessert.

The Napkin

At an informal or formal meal, the napkin is placed either on the plate or to the left of the flatware—never under it. If you're doing a fancy fold, you'll undoubtedly want to show it off by putting it right on the plate.

Plates

Plates are easiest of all to deal with because they come and go with the courses. The dinner plate will usually be on the table, at the center of the place setting, when you sit down. It may be resting on a larger plate called a charger—these are fashionable now, but purely ornamental. The bread-and-butter plate will also be in place, to the left and above the dinner plate as shown on page 176. If a salad plate is on the table, it will be placed on, or to the left of, the dinner plate. It is usually removed after the salad is eaten. The first-course plate will either be resting on a larger plate, with food on it, when you sit down or it will be brought in with the course—and then removed. The soup bowl and plate also may be in place (if this is the first course), or it will be brought in when the course is served and then taken away afterward.

SOUP TO NUTS: COURSES YOU'RE LIKELY TO ENCOUNTER

Here are some tips on eating your way through the various courses of a meal.

Seafood

This catch-all category includes clams and oysters on the half shell as well as shrimp. A small seafood fork is used to eat all these foods, but if you're given a salad or entrée fork, use that instead. Leave the fork on the serving plate when finished. Shrimp with the tails still attached may be eaten with your fingers.

Fish

Use the fish fork and knife, if one is provided. Leave both on the plate when finished. When fish is served as an entrée instead of a separate course, you usually use the place fork and knife. If the fish is bony, you're allowed to pick at it— delicately, of course—with your fork and knife. In fact, the fish fork and knife are designed with this in mind. You may use your fingers to discreetly remove any small bones.

Soup

Move the soup spoon from front to back as you eat soup. Eat as quietly as possible. Slurping, a compliment to the cook in many Asian cultures, is considered bad form in the West. You may tip the bowl away from you slightly to finish a soup. Leave the spoon on the serving plate when you have finished or in a wide, flat soup bowl—but never in the smaller consommé bowl.

Salad

Use the salad fork to eat salad. If the greens are not bite-sized, first try to cut them with the fork. If necessary, use a knife. Leave the salad fork and knife on the plate when finished. You will either be brought a new knife to use in eating your entrée or asked to keep the one you have.

Entrée

Use the large place fork and knife to eat the main course. Leave your utensils completely on your plate when finished. They should not rest half on and half off.

Fruit

Now that fruit is being served more often in place of dessert, Americans seem to be eating it more formally—that is, with a knife and fork. At minimum, it's polite to use a knife to cut fruit into smaller pieces, which you may then eat with your fingers. If the fruit is at all soft or messy, as persimmons and mangoes are, for example, then cut it into bite-sized pieces and eat it with a fork.

Dessert

Depending upon what's served, use a fork or a spoon, occasionally both. Pie à la mode, for example, requires both.

FAMILY STYLE VS. FOOD SERVED IN COURSES

Most meals are served either family style or in courses. Family style means that all—or almost all—the food is put on the table at the same time and then passed to everyone present.

Passing food counterclockwise makes it easier for the mostly right-handed world to serve itself, but the trick is simply to pass all the food in any one direction. If you start passing it, send it counterclockwise. If someone else starts passing food clockwise, then by all means follow suit to avoid confusion.

When a meal is served in courses, the host or servers will bring it out on plates or serving platters and present it to each diner. When served this way, food is presented on the diner's left and removed, if possible, from the right. You may serve yourself using large serving utensils, or you may be served.

RESTING VS. DONE POSITIONS

Between bites you may put down your utensils—on your plate, please, never on the table. Make sure your utensils are completely on your plate, not half on and half off.

Placing the knife and fork, tines up or down, whichever you prefer, together on your plate at the four o'clock position, as shown opposite (bottom) signals the waiter that you're done eating and not merely resting between bites as shown opposite (top). The four o'clock position is a convenience to the person who's clearing since it leaves the top part of the plate free to pick up.

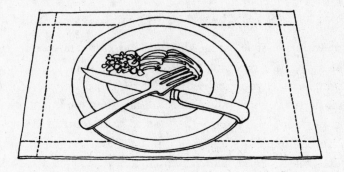

RESTING POSITION

FINISHED POSITION

AMERICAN VS. CONTINENTAL EATING STYLES

In American-style eating, the fork and knife are used to cut off a bite-size piece of food. The knife, which is in your right hand as you cut, is then put on the plate, the fork is transferred to your right hand, and it is then used, in a tines-up position, to transport the food to the mouth.

In continental-style eating, the knife and fork are used to cut a bite of food, which is then transported on the fork, tines down and in your left hand, to the mouth. The knife, which may be used to secure the food on the back of the fork, stays in your right hand. Left-handers may reverse this process.

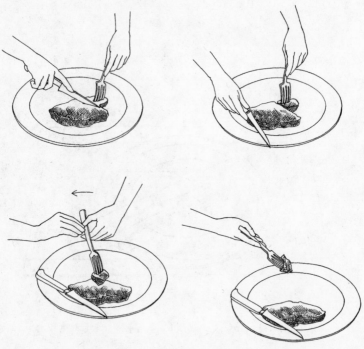

AMERICAN-STYLE EATING

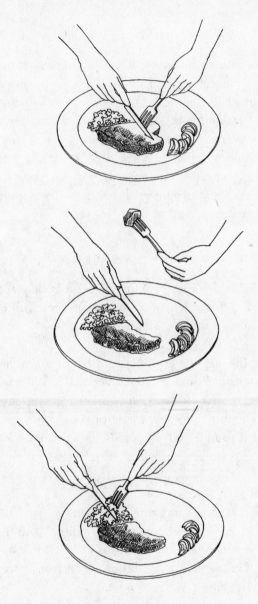

CONTINENTAL-STYLE EATING

USED FLATWARE

Once you have used a piece of flatware, replace it on a plate. Sometimes, though, you'll be asked to keep some flatware when your plate is removed from the table. When this happens, the best solution is to position it in a large place spoon, if there is one, or to put it on the butter plate. Only as a last option should you put it on the table, especially if there is a tablecloth. And never, ever should you use your napkin to wipe it clean before putting it down, however practical an idea this may seem to be.

USING A NAPKIN

When you sit down, a napkin will be at your place, either on the plate, to the left of it, or perhaps folded into a glass. Here are some hints on napkin use:

• Put the napkin in your lap as soon as you're settled into your chair or after grace has been said. You may unfold it completely or not, but don't shake it out ostentatiously, and don't tuck it into any article of your clothing.

• Use it to blot your lips lightly before taking a drink in order to remove any unsightly crumbs that might cling to the glass.

• Blot your lips between courses.

• Use it to cover unsightly occurrences—such as the removal of a piece of gristle you can't swallow. (But there's no need to be too prissy about this: it's okay, for example, to remove a cherry pit or other small seed from your mouth without shielding it with a napkin.)

• Don't use it as a handkerchief, no matter how desperate you are.

• Don't use it to stash that piece of meat you couldn't chew. Discreetly place the meat on your plate, hiding it if possible under a lettuce leaf or some other food so as to make it as inconspicuous as possible.

• Do replace the napkin, when you're done using it, to the left of your plate or where the plate was if it has already been cleared. Don't refold it as if it hasn't been used, and don't crumple it up.

Finger Bowls and Hot Napkins

Finger bowls are seen only at formal dinners and some restaurants, where they are given to diners who have eaten an especially messy food such as lobster or ribs. The correct way to use one is to dip your fingers into the bowl and then dry them off, usually below table level, on your napkin or on the special napkin or hot cloth provided with the bowl.

Akin to finger bowls are the hot napkins that are sometimes served in Asian restaurants and on airplanes. You are expected to use them to clean your hands before the meal. On an airplane you may, of course, feel free not to use one, but at an Asian restaurant and especially in someone's home, it's rude not to do so even if you've just washed your hands. To use one, unwrap the towel, rub it over your hands, and then replace it, still unfolded, beside your plate or on the small presentation tray.

STARTING THE MEAL

When the hostess or host announces that dinner is served, everyone should move toward the table as soon as possible. The food is ready and hot, and it's polite to move quickly to the table.

The hostess may have a specified seating arrangement in

mind, or she may let guests sit wherever they like. Either way, the polite guest waits for some direction from her. If there are place cards, walk around until you find the one with your name on it; that's where you sit. Contrary to the funny stories you may have heard about switching place cards, it's rude to do this even at a very large party. Usually a great deal of thought has gone into arranging the seating, and a hostess quite rightfully will be upset to have her planning undone by an uncaring guest.

Some families say grace, so don't put your napkin in your lap (or, worse, begin to eat) until your hosts have had an opportunity to say it. If it is said, bow your head politely and listen attentively.

The custom is for the hostess to take the first bite, but if she urges her guests to go ahead and eat, then they should. She might, for example, be busy in the kitchen for a few more minutes or might be filling each plate at the table, and thus your food would get cold were you to wait for her to begin eating.

MINDING YOUR TABLE MANNERS

When You Must Leave the Table

There are occasions when leaving the table is the polite thing to do, even if a meal is in progress. If you're chewing something unchewable (a piece of gristly meat, for example), you may have to make a quick trip to the kitchen or bathroom to wrap it in a paper towel and dispose of it.

If a coughing or sneezing fit suddenly strikes, it's polite to take care of it somewhere else. The same is true of belching or hiccups. A sudden attack of illness also may call for you to leave the table. Even a fit of laughter, if it gets out of hand, may necessitate a brief respite in another room.

When any of these things happens, excuse yourself—with your eyes if you can't speak—and leave. Then return as soon as you've gotten yourself together. Try not to be absent too long, as it does interrupt the pace of the meal, and others will worry about you.

Give some brief excuse for leaving so the other diners know everything is all right. Details are not required. Simply say, for example, "Sorry, not feeling well. Be right back." Some things, hiccups or a laughing fit, are self-explanatory, and no one will worry about you.

Choking

The one time when you absolutely must not leave the table—because you need other people to save your life—is when you are choking on a piece of food. Before the Heimlich maneuver was invented, unbelievable as this may seem, polite people actually excused themselves and left the room when they were choking. Now we know this is absolutely the wrong thing to do.

If you are choking, you won't be able to speak. Putting your hand to your throat is the universal gesture indicating that you need help. If you think someone is choking, ask him if he can speak, and if he indicates no, one person should perform the Heimlich maneuver while someone else calls for medical help.

A poster demonstrating the Heimlich maneuver is posted at most restaurants, and we should all take some time to study it every now and then.

Reaching

Most of us think of reaching for food as a definite faux pas. We make a small grab for something and then offer a grandiose apology, when, in fact, a little polite reaching is better than none at all. Consider this: When you ask for food to be passed, someone has to stop eating, put down her utensils, and pick up a dish to hand it to you. That's why it's sometimes better to reach.

But what's a polite reach? Generally, if food is within a short arm's length of you, and you don't have to pass your arm in front of anyone's body or venture into a diner's place setting, it's more polite to reach than to ask.

There are also times not to reach for something even though you could. If the salt and pepper shakers, for example, are sitting right by someone's plate, you must assume they are about to be used, and thus you should ask if you may have them. Then they will be handed to you.

Posture at the Table

As long as you don't slouch, or look as if the table is holding you up, it's perfectly acceptable to rest an elbow (or even two) on the table, especially between courses. In a restaurant the only way to hear your fellow diners may be to put both elbows on the table and lean forward.

Cutting up Food

Unless you're under two years of age and your mother or father is cutting up your food, you should cut one bite at a time. The only exception is a physically impaired adult, who might find it more efficient to cut all his food at once, especially if someone else is helping out. (But remember to wait for the other person to ask for your assistance or indicate what he wants done; it's never polite to take the lead in a situation like this.)

Spilled and Dropped Food

When you spill or drop food, unless it needs an immediate cleanup, the polite thing to do is—nothing. If you're eating at someone's house, *after* the meal is over you can discreetly call the food to the hostess's attention or pick it up yourself. In a restaurant, let it be. If you've dropped a utensil, quietly ask for a replacement.

The main reason to refrain from immediate action is that it is less disruptive to the table. Your host usually has his hands full orchestrating the meal, so unless you've dumped red wine on the carpet, don't interrupt the flow.

If you must call your host's attention to something—because you *did* spill red wine on the carpet, for example—then let him take care of it. He knows what he wants to use to clean up or even whether he wants to clean up now or later. The same rules apply in a restaurant. The staff is there to wait on you, so let them do their jobs.

The only exception here is when you are with young children. Given a choice, most hosts and restaurant staff would prefer that you not let your child make a mess. Failing this, they would like an offer to clean up—which most of the time they'll decline, if they're polite. Rarely would they like you to actually go to work cleaning up, but if you can't stop yourself, then limit the cleanup to wiping away obvious crumbs in seating areas, as well as any liquid spills, and perhaps drawing someone's attention to any special problems. And then an apology is nice.

If you're eating in someone's home with small children,

you should always follow the hostess's lead. If she wants to feed the children in the kitchen or at a separate table, that's her prerogative. Your children may always eat with you at home, but in someone else's home you do it their way. And they return the favor when they visit you.

Pests in Food

Should you encounter an unwanted pest in your food, try to draw as little attention to it as possible. You'll undoubtedly be revolted, but that's not something you need to share with your neighbors. Quietly say to whoever is serving, "I think I need another bowl of soup." The food will be replaced at once. If you're sitting next to someone who has this problem, ignore it. It's not polite to ask what has happened or otherwise draw attention to the situation. If you realize that someone hasn't noticed a problem with his food, mention it to him quietly.

Sharing Food

When eating in a restaurant, you'll occasionally want to share food. In even the finest restaurants people share food these days, so if you know in advance that this is what you'll be doing, ask for an extra plate when you order.

If you haven't planned in advance, the best way to share a meal is for the person who is being offered the food to pass a plate (usually the butter plate) across the table. The person with the food then cuts off a piece, transfers it to the plate, and returns it.

There are also some ways *not* to share food: Don't pass a piece of food across the table. It's almost sure to drip on the tablecloth. Don't reach across the table with your fork or spoon to retrieve a piece of someone's food. That's really

tacky and will almost certainly leave a telltale and embarrassing trail on the tablecloth.

Table Talk

It's hard to imagine in these days of excessive television vio-
lence that some subjects are still taboo at the table, but nevertheless, a few are. In fact, most of what's on the evening
news isn't fit for discussion at a dinner table: illness, surgical
and medical procedures, grisly crimes, death, and anything
disturbing about food (such as a television exposé of poultry)
are generally not subjects anyone will want to hear about
over dinner.

It's also impolite to bring up anything controversial at the
table, although what's controversial may vary from one
household to the next or with the company. Generally, dis-
cussions about politics or religion are considered taboo. The
exception, though, is the occasional hostess who encourages
and even thrives on spirited conversation at her table.

Victorian hostesses used to tap on a glass in order to "turn
the table." When this happened, diners stopped—practically
in midsentence—and began talking to the person on their
other side. Although hostesses no longer formally turn the
table, it's still polite to talk at some point during a dinner to
the people seated on both sides of you. A good icebreaker is
to ask how they know the hostess or to solicit their opinion
of something the table has been discussing.

Smoking

Smoking is less tolerated these days at the dinner table and in
many homes. Small ashtrays used to arrive with the coffee,
but no longer. Here's how to handle smoking when you are
a dinner guest:

- If there are no ashtrays on the table, assume you can't smoke. It's better not to ask.
- If ashtrays are on the table, you must still ask before you light up.
- Never smoke before everyone at the table has finished eating. Smoke interferes with the taste of food.
- If you do smoke around nonsmokers, be as careful as possible. Direct the smoke away from everyone present, and keep smoking to a minimum.

TEN TRICKY FOODS AND HOW TO EAT THEM

You're at the apex of your social skills when you feel free to tackle a food you've never eaten before—in front of others, no less. Here are some tips to help you attain this lofty perch:

1. Oysters and clams. These are typically served on the half shell on a plate of ice and are eaten with a seafood fork. After dressing the shellfish with whatever condiments you prefer, hold the shell in place with one hand and use the fork to pick up the meat. You can pick up the shell and drain the liquid if you like.

2. Snails. These are difficult to eat only when they're served in the shell. You'll be supplied a pair of tongs whose sole purpose is to hold the snail shell while you use the seafood fork to lift out the delicacy and transport it to your mouth. You're wondering what can go wrong? Well, should you fail to get the tongs wrapped around the shell just right, you may find yourself among the countless first-time snail eaters who have flipped a snail across the room. It's embarrassing, and the best way to avoid this is to work *very* care-

EATING SNAILS

fully to position those tongs securely around the shell before you attempt to eat it (see illustration above).

An alternate—and more surefire—method is to pick up the shell with your napkin. Most of us are reluctant to put a cloth napkin to this use, yet it is entirely appropriate to do so. In fact, you could not use a paper napkin in this way without burning your hands, since snails in the shell are cooked in a special dish and brought to the table bubbling hot from the oven. Therefore, holding the *cloth* napkin in one hand, use the other to work the seafood fork into the shell, then retrieve the snail and convey it to your mouth.

1. PULL OFF THE LARGE CLAWS, AND IF THEY
HAVE NOT BEEN CRACKED IN THE KITCHEN,
USE THE NUTCRACKER TO CRACK THEM. THIS
LETS YOU GET TO THE MEAT INSIDE.

2. PULL THE TAIL AWAY FROM THE REST OF
THE BODY.

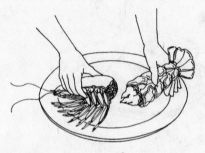

3. USING YOUR FORK, PULL THE TAIL MEAT
OUT OF THE SHELL IN ONE PIECE, SO IT CAN
BE EATEN WITH A KNIFE AND FORK.

3.   Lobster. Sometimes the large shells of a lobster will be cracked in the kitchen before they're brought to you. You can also ask that this be done. If the shells are not cracked, the lobster will be served with a utensil that looks like a nutcracker. Pull off the large claws and use the utensil to crack them. Use the seafood fork to dig out the meat in the large claws. Next, separate the tail, which contains most of the meat, from the body. You can either slip the meat entirely out of the shell, as shown opposite, and use a knife and fork to eat it as you would any other piece of food, or you can leave it in the shell and eat it with the seafood fork while holding down the shell with your other hand. Finally, you may pick up the small claws with your fingers and either dig out (with the cocktail fork) or suck out the meat. Place the discarded shells on your plate. The coral-colored roe and soft green liver are edible and are, in fact, considered delicacies.

In an informal lobster restaurant you'll often be given a bib to wear as you eat. They're very convenient, and there's no reason not to use one.

4.   Artichokes. Start at the bottom. Pull off the tender, large leaves with your fingers, dip them in whatever sauce is provided, and scrape the meaty, concave side against your teeth. Discard the leaves on the serving plate under the artichoke or on the special bowl or plate that is provided for them.

After working your way through the leaves in this manner, you'll reach the tough, inedible thistle, which you must conquer to get to the real delicacy—the heart. Hold down the artichoke with your fork and gently place your knife at about a forty-five-degree angle, pointed downward. Work your way around the thistle, cutting it out. You'll be left with the concave surface of the artichoke's heart. Cut it into bite-size pieces, dip it in sauce, and enjoy this luscious pièce de résistance.

5.   Frog's legs. These midwestern delicacies are eaten much like chicken legs. Use a knife and fork to break the leg into two pieces at the joint. Eat as much of the meat as you can with your knife and fork; then use your fingers to continue. Put the bones on your plate.

6.   Olive oil. A plate or small bowl of olive oil is showing up in lots of places these days, in lieu of butter for bread. If you're dining solo, you may of course dip directly into the oil, but when dining with others, spoon some oil onto your bread plate and then dip your bread into it.

7.   Pasta. Although Americans have eaten pasta for generations, we haven't completely resolved how to eat it, especially when it comes in the long, stringy form. (Obviously small pastas that can be eaten with a fork pose no problem.) Pasta is often served with a large spoon. Take a smallish portion of pasta on your fork, then hold your fork against the spoon and wrap until you've formed a neat mouthful. You can also do the same thing without a spoon, by holding a fork against the side of the pasta bowl or plate and wrapping against it.

8.   Kiwi. This little fruit is now ubiquitous in American grocery stores, primarily because it travels so well. Often you'll be served kiwi that's already been peeled and sliced, in which case you need eat it only with a fork. But more and more it is showing up in its unpeeled, slightly furry state. Kiwi is soft, so peel it carefully with a knife, holding it in your hand as you go. Replace it on your plate, and use your knife and fork to cut it into small, bite-size pieces. (At a very casual dinner, you may want to hold it in your hand and quarter it with a knife, then eat it from your fingers.)

9.   Mango. The skins are not edible, but they make an excellent cup. Cut the fruit in half, and use a spoon to eat the fruit out of the skin.

10.   Persimmon. This delicious fall fruit should be placed

stem side down and cut into quarters. Then use your knife and fork to cut it into small bites. Alternately, you can cut it in half like a mango and scoop out the flesh. Persimmons are too soft to peel.

A Foolproof Method for Dealing with New Foods

Finally, there is a special tip that will help you get through those times when a strange or exotic food finds its way to your plate, leaving you with a sinking feeling—because you haven't the slightest idea how to eat it. The tip is simple: wait for your hostess to start and then follow her lead.

HOWEVER YOU EAT, TRY TO REMEMBER THAT THE REAL purpose of table manners is to make dining an enjoyable and aesthetic experience for everyone present at the table. As an added bonus, they help build your social confidence. With good table manners, you can eat comfortably anywhere in the world.

Chapter 8

CORRESPONDENCE AND PROTOCOL

FEW OF US ACTUALLY WRITE LETTERS ANYMORE, THANKS to that great invention—the telephone. However there are still a few occasions when only a written note or letter will do. And for those times, you will need some nice writing paper.

STATIONERY

Stationery is sold at office supply stores, card shops, and at some jewelers, although the latter tend to specialize in engraved stationery, which is more expensive than other kinds. It comes in a variety of sizes, styles, and colors, ranging from full-size paper in white or ivory that is used in formal and business correspondence to colorful preprinted note cards suitable for informal exchanges.

The largest-size writing paper is 8½ by 11 inches, which

works well for typewritten and handwritten correspondence. Many people also find it useful to keep on hand a supply of 3-by-5-inch folded notepaper called informals. Ironically, informals are most often used these days for our "formal" correspondence, such as thank-you and condolence notes. Even if you like the colorful, stylish informals, it's a good idea to stock a conservative notepaper for those times when colorful stationery is inappropriate.

Stationery can be expensive, but there are also plenty of attractive, inexpensive papers from which to choose. What makes writing paper expensive is the content of the paper (rag costs more than wood fiber) and the engraving or printing process, although printing is considerably less expensive than engraving. A perfectly acceptable box of unengraved, wood-fiber paper can cost as little as four dollars, while rag paper, engraved, can cost hundreds.

Printed and Engraved Stationery

Many people enjoy having engraved or printed stationery. The custom of engraving one's name on stationery probably began when people stopped using a wax seal on correspondence but still wanted to incorporate a personal touch.

Engraving is expensive, especially the first time it is ordered, since a special plate is cut for each order. But once a plate is made, it can be used repeatedly, provided you don't need to change your letterhead. Printing is much less expensive, and printing processes have improved so much that printed stationery now rivals engraved in quality.

Whether stationery is printed or engraved, it usually includes a person's name and address. If the paper will be used for business, telephone and fax numbers are also included, and we are already beginning to see e-mail addresses on stationery as well.

By tradition and because it's too small to do much else, an informal is printed only with a name or monogram. The address goes on the envelope.

HANDWRITTEN CORRESPONDENCE

Most letters can be typed or, as is more often the case, churned out by a computer's printer. Only thank-you and condolence notes must be handwritten, although if there is a physical reason you can't handwrite such a note, a type-written note is, of course, acceptable—and better than nothing.

If you have the time and are so inclined, it's especially gracious to send handwritten notes of congratulations, encouragement, and praise to friends and acquaintances. Such correspondence helps to expand one's circle of friends, cultivate acquaintances, and stay in touch with family members.

Thank-You Notes

Almost any time someone gives you a gift, you owe her a written thank-you note. The only exceptions are hostess gifts and gifts exchanged among very good friends and family members who see each other regularly. In these instances you have the chance to thank the giver personally when you open the gift and also to tell her again the next time you see her how much you like the present. But apart from these exceptions, thank-you notes must be written for all of the more formal gift-giving occasions—birthdays, weddings, anniversaries, and so on.

Thank-you notes can be written on informals or regular-size stationery, whichever you prefer. Since these are happy-occasion notes, the paper can be as colorful and decorative as you like, and colored inks are acceptable as well.

A thank-you note should mention the gift specifically and tell why you like it or how you plan to use it. Apart from this, it can be brief. For example, it might read as follows:

> Dear Grandma,
> Thank you for the lovely etched glass plate. It will be especially handy at holiday time, and I can already see it filled with cookies. It's exactly what we needed, and Ben and I both thank you so much for remembering our anniversary.
> Love,
> Susie

Isn't this far better than saying, "Thank you for the plate"?

Sooner or later we are all faced with writing a thank-you note for a gift we don't particularly like or may even hate. You needn't lie when you find yourself in this situation, but you should certainly try to find something nice to say about the present.

Let's say, for example, that your Aunt Sally has given you a sweater you wouldn't be caught dead wearing. You don't like it, nor does it like you. Frankly, you're going to pass it on to someone else at the first opportunity. But it is in a decent—well, okay, a downright acceptable—shade of pink, one you look quite nice wearing.

Here is the really important thing to keep in mind: Your Aunt Sally meant well when she bought the sweater. She spent her time and money choosing something she hoped you would like, and it's not her fault the choice was less than perfect for you. Therefore your obligation is to write a thank-you note that acknowledges the spirit in which the gift was given. It might read like this:

> *Dear Aunt Sally,*
> *It was really sweet of you to remember my fifteenth birthday.*
> *The sweater is the most beautiful shade of pink I've ever seen.*
> *As I'm sure you know, this color is really hot right now.*
> *Thanks again for remembering me with such a generous present.*
> *Love,*
> *Eliza*

It's never polite, regardless of the circumstances, to tell someone that you dislike a present, that you already own it, or that you will not be wearing or using it. Thank-you notes should leave the receiver feeling good for having bought you a present. They should also be sent as soon as possible, within days rather than weeks, after receiving a gift.

Condolence Notes

The purpose of a condolence note is to offer sympathy to a friend or acquaintance who has lost a loved one. These, too, must be handwritten. The only exceptions are notes sent to business colleagues, which may be typed on your business stationery. Condolence notes are written on plain white or cream-colored paper, either an informal or larger-size stationery. Either blue or black ink is appropriate.

Many people dread writing condolence notes because they don't know what to say, but in reality you can say very little and still show your concern. The important thing is to let the person know how deeply you care about his or her loss. For example, the briefest kind of sympathy note, the kind you might write when you know the mourner but perhaps not the person who died, might read like this:

> Dear Joan,
> Frank and I just want to let you know how sad we feel about your loss. You are in our thoughts. Please let us know if we can do anything for you.
> Love,
> Maria

A more extended condolence note, one written about someone you knew well, might recall the last time you were together with the person who died or some other enjoyable moment you shared. Mourners are especially comforted to hear about other people's experiences with their loved one.

Two questions that often arise are when and to whom you should send a condolence note. The answer is that you may send one any time you hear of someone's death, even if a year or two has elapsed. And you should send a note whenever it feels right to do so. The recipient doesn't have to be a close friend or someone you see regularly. It is comforting to hear from people when you have lost someone dear to you, and no one is ever ungrateful to receive a caring message of concern.

Another question I often hear is whether one can send a commercial condolence card. These seem to become more popular with each passing year. A handwritten personal note is always preferred, but if you find you simply can't write one or are incapacitated physically in a way that makes it impossible to do so, then any kind of card—even a preprinted one—is better than nothing.

Answering Condolence Notes

When someone takes the time to write a condolence note, the recipient should send a thank-you note in reply. It is only marginally acceptable to send the preprinted thank-you notes supplied by funeral directors (and then only if you are swamped with mail), but these should be followed up with personally written thank-you notes. Best of all, though, is to skip the preprinted notes in favor of a personal reply. Strictly speaking, you need not send a handwritten note in response to a preprinted condolence card, but it's kind to do so. After all, the thought was there.

Although it may initially seem like a tedious business to answer all the condolence notes you receive, there are two good reasons to do so, and only one has anything to do with etiquette. People expend considerable emotional energy writing condolence notes. Since these are never easy to write, they deserve a personal response. The other reason to write thank-you notes is that they can be part of the healing process. Just as others express their sadness over the loss by writing a condolence note, the bereaved person can, in some small way, express his by responding.

Just-to-Be-Nice Notes

There is no better way to build and enrich friendships than to send notes for special occasions—or no occasion at all. Think about sending a brief note to someone who has been promoted or has received some other honor. Or send one to someone who helped you out in a special way, by serving on a committee with you or assisting with another project. Notes can go to anyone you deem worthy of praise. This kind of communication builds bridges by making others feel good, and I truly believe good feelings like these come back to us sooner or later in one form or another.

These little notes can be written with the brightest-colored ink on your prettiest or most festive paper. They can be handwritten or typewritten, although the former always feels more personal. Such notes needn't be long. A few lines congratulating your friend on her achievement, honor, or kind deed will more than suffice.

INVITATIONS

Formal Invitations

Occasionally we receive formal invitations, most typically to weddings but sometimes to anniversary parties or other kinds of galas. A formal invitation is printed (or engraved) on cream or white paper and worded as follows:

MR. AND MRS. WILLIAM JONES
REQUEST THE HONOR OF YOUR COMPANY
AT THE MARRIAGE OF THEIR DAUGHTER
SUSANNAH MARIE
TO
MR. ANTHONY WINSTON
SATURDAY, THE TWENTY-SECOND OF JUNE
AT HALF PAST FOUR O'CLOCK
ST. BARTHOLOMEW'S CHURCH
HOUSTON
AND AFTERWARD AT THE RECEPTION
HOUSTON ATHLETIC CLUB

Some Words about the Wording

Note the invitation requests the "honor of your company" if the wedding (or event) is held in a church or synagogue. If it is held elsewhere, the invitation should request the "pleasure of your company."

Formal invitations require a response whether it is asked for specifically or not. Most invitations do ask for a response, either in French, with the letters "RSVP" *(Répondez, s'il vous plaît,* meaning "Respond, please") or the simpler English wording "Please respond." Both are correct.

The New Formal Invitation

Traditionally, formal invitations have been covered with a piece of tissue (an artifact of the days of long-drying engraving inks) and mailed with two envelopes. But with today's quick-drying inks, the tissue no longer serves a purpose, and in these days of ecological concern, the extra envelope seems wasteful. You may now send even the most formal invitation without a tissue and in only one envelope.

Enclosures with a Formal Wedding Invitation

If everyone is invited to both the wedding and the reception, then the reception information can be printed on the invitation. If more people are invited to the ceremony than to the reception, separate reception cards are inserted in the invitations of those who are invited to attend both. The card should read as follows:

RECEPTION

IMMEDIATELY FOLLOWING THE CEREMONY

HOUSTON ATHLETIC CLUB

RSVP

Other enclosures that sometimes come in formal invitations are reply cards (see page 212) and pew cards, which direct you to a specific pew and are used only for large, very formal weddings. Hotel and tourist information, as well as directions, should be mailed separately.

Responding to a Formal Invitation—or Any Invitation

Any time you receive an invitation, formal or otherwise, with or without a request to reply, you are expected to let the sender know—in a timely fashion—whether or not you will be able to attend the event. Judging from the number of complaints I receive from brides and their mothers, some of us don't realize how important a timely response is. A caterer can't make final plans, nor can the price of an event be determined, until a final head count has been established. As a general rule, events elaborate enough to require a formal invitation are expensive.

If you receive a formal invitation that does not include a reply card, you should reply in kind—that is, on a similar white or cream-colored card or stationery, but in your own handwriting. Your response should echo the formal wording of the invitation. For example:

Mr. and Mrs. Amiel Craig
accept with pleasure★
the kind invitation of
Mr. and Mrs. William Jones
for
Saturday, the twenty-second of June

You should note the day and date, but need not repeat the time or the place.

★ or alternately: "regret they are unable to accept"

If you're uncomfortable with this format, perhaps because you're an old family friend, you can relay your acceptance or regrets on a plain informal. Best of all, however, is to answer formally and then send along a separate note saying how happy you are to be included and how much you're looking forward to attending.

Once you've accepted an invitation, whether written or not, you are obligated to attend the event. Only if there is a death or major illness should you bow out. If you must cancel at the last minute, you may telephone rather than sending a note.

Reply Cards

We may not like reply cards but most of us recognize the need for them. Unfortunately, so many people do not reply to formal invitations, or do not reply in time, that these cards have become a necessity, and no one should be embarrassed to use them.

If you do use them, be sure they really work for you. Specify a deadline for replying (usually at least two weeks before you have to lock in the caterer and other suppliers) and also leave a blank line where the recipient can write in the number of people who will be attending.

Incidentally, the number who will be attending can't exceed the number invited. Some people erroneously believe their children or other household members are included in formal invitations. In fact, the only people invited are those to whom the invitation is addressed. If an invitation is directed only to you and your husband, it does not include your children, no matter how young or how old they may be. And it's rude to call the hostess to ask if they may attend.

Reply cards are always sent with preaddressed, stamped envelopes.

Invitations to an Informal Wedding

Invitations to an informal wedding may be printed, hand-written, or telephoned, especially when time is short. They may be on white or colored stock and may contain informal wording, a poem, or other artistic expressions. If handwritten, they might read like this:

> Dear Joan,
> Sally and Jim are being married in a small, quiet ceremony on Saturday, June 30, at 4 p.m. at St. Christopher's on Twelfth Street. We hope you'll be able to join us for this and a small reception afterward.
> Love,
> Marie

Informal Invitations

Informal invitations that are used for birthday parties, anniversaries, and other celebrations may be specially printed, or you can buy preprinted cards and fill in the pertinent information.

Like formal invitations, informals require a response even when this isn't stated specifically on the invitation. If a telephone number is included on the RSVP line, then you can respond by phone.

A Word about Nontraditional Wedding Invitations

Nontraditional wedding invitations seem to have found their niche, and one now sees even very formal invitations printed on pastel stock with untraditional wording and design. Some are personalized in interesting ways that still compass the bounds of tradition, while others veer far from conventional taste. Before choosing a nontraditional wedding invitation, consider two things:

First, you may be giving your guests the impression that your wedding is a much less formal event than it actually will be. Second, the invitation may not stand the test of time. If this matters to you, you may want to think twice before including outlandish art or sentimental songs or verses. These can come back to haunt you later.

Dress and Formal Invitations

Formal invitations often state the kind of dress that is requested—that is, either black tie or white tie. In the absence of this information, you can usually judge from the invitation how formal an event will be, or you can make inquiries of the host or others who are invited.

A formal invitation implies that the dress is at least black tie, and most invitations note if white tie is requested. Dress varies from one region of the country to another and even from community to community, but black tie typically means tuxedos or dark dressy suits for men and short evening wear (cocktail dresses) for women. White tie means a tailcoat and its accoutrements for men and long or very dressy short evening gowns for women.

COMMERCIAL GREETING CARDS

The commercial greeting card business is booming and I fear, contributing to our failure to write each other truly personal notes. We can now even apologize via a preprinted card, and I'm not sure that's good. Still, many of these cards are wonderfully clever and witty and can serve a definite purpose. Certainly a preprinted card is better than nothing.

About the only time they are unacceptable, as was noted earlier, is for thank-you and condolence notes.

If you use commercial cards, do exercise some caution in making your selection. Cards range from the unctuous and saccharine to the totally sarcastic, and what looks funny when you're standing in a store may not always strike the recipient the same way. A good alternative to cards with preprinted messages are commercial cards without messages. You supply your own—message, that is. Some of these cards are quite lovely and tasteful, and they work well.

HOLIDAY GREETING CARDS

Holiday cards, whether for Christmas, Chanukah, or some other occasion, are a good way to stay in touch with friends and relatives and to wish everyone a happy holiday season.

Many holiday cards have a religious theme, and I'm often asked whether it's appropriate to send a card with a religious theme to someone of a different faith. The answer is that it is not. If you will be sending cards to people of other religions at holiday time, either buy one that honors the recipient's holiday or buy a more generic card. Messages that read "Happy Holidays," "Have a Happy Holiday," or "Season's Greetings" are considered generic (in place of "Merry Christmas" or "Happy Chanukah"), and "Happy New Year" is acceptable as well.

Many people also aren't clear on what constitutes a religious card. Cards depicting obvious symbols of a religion— menorahs or scrolls for Jews, and nativities, Wise Men, and stars of Bethlehem for Christians—should not be sent to people of other faiths. Keep in mind that even though Christmas trees, wreaths and Santa Claus may just seem to be signs of the winter season, they are, in fact, part of the

Christmas tradition. Winter scenes, domestic scenes, and doves (for peace) are all appropriate on ecumenical cards.

Printed Holiday Cards

If your holiday list is very long (or even if it isn't), it's acceptable to send cards printed with your name. When you do this, though, it's a nice warm touch to add a handwritten message.

Signing Holiday Cards

Most people like to sign the names of all family members but aren't sure about the correct order. Traditionally the order is the husband's name, the wife's name, and the names of the children, from oldest to youngest. Alternately, you may adhere to the courtesy of signing your partner's name first, which of course means the signatures will vary depending upon who has written the cards. Every year I get a few cards that have been signed by every member of the family, and I find these especially charming.

Sending Cards to Those in Mourning

Holiday cards may be sent to people in mourning. But send a more subdued card or, better yet, write a personal note of holiday greetings.

In our society we try to get mourning out of the way as quickly as possible, which means we often don't acknowledge how hard the holidays can be on the recently bereaved. But it's sometimes better to send a note that openly acknowledges this isn't the usual cheery holiday season for a friend. You can say something like "I realize this won't be the best of holidays for you, but I want you to know I'm thinking of you and hoping you will find some cheer in the season despite your loss." Anyone going through his first holiday season without a loved one will be having an especially rough time—and will appreciate your special consideration.

Christmas Letters

People either love holiday letters from friends or they abhor them. The problem with most letters is that they're badly written. I'm speaking here not of writing style, which can easily be forgiven, but of content. If you're determined to send a holiday letter, don't drag family and friends through your entire year, reporting month by month on minutiae in your life.

Instead go for the highlights: who graduated, who got promoted, who moved, who had babies. Also, in hitting the highlights, try not to brag. In fact, if you discover upon examining your motives that you seem more interested in showcasing what you've done than spreading goodwill to your friends, think twice about sending a letter. Finally, even if you send a form letter (and that's what these are), try to add a handwritten word or two—just to personalize it.

PERSONAL BUSINESS CORRESPONDENCE

On occasion we all need to write a personal business letter. We must notify a credit card company of a change of address or write a letter of complaint to a store. We write politicians or other public officials to express our opinions, and less often, we write to praise someone—a clerk who went out of her way to help us or a public official who provided some special service.

For this kind of correspondence, personal business stationery is appropriate. Look for white, cream, buff, or gray paper, $8^{1}/_{2}$ by 11 inches or slightly smaller. You can have it imprinted with your name and address or plain. If necessary, a good typing or computer paper will suffice. It is most helpful if your business stationery is printed with your name and address, but if you don't use it often enough to warrant this expense, then buy plain stationery and type your return address (street, city, state, and zip code) under the date. This should either be centered on the page or positioned off to the right.

The format of a business letter differs from one of social correspondence. A business letter contains a formal heading and a greeting. Here is a sample business letter:

July 2, 1996

Stretch-Time Exercise Clothes
30 Circle Drive
Plainfield, Indiana 46168

Dear Sir or Ma'am:
I am writing to complain about a leotard I recently ordered from your company. After four washings, it began to fall apart at the seams. I enclose the garment so you can see what I mean. I would like a refund of my money, as per your offer of a money-back guarantee. I shall be most appreciative of your attention to this matter.

Sincerely,
Marylou Steffens

The Heading

The heading consists of the date, usually centered on the page, and the name and address of the person to whom you're writing. Formal titles, if applicable, are used.

The Greeting

The greeting often poses the biggest problem when writing a business letter. What do you call someone you've never met, someone whose sex you do not know? The best greeting in these cases is the simplest one. Write "Dear Sir or Ma'am," which at least has the advantage of covering all bases. When you know someone's name, by all means use it, but use the entire name until you are on a first-name basis.

The Body of the Letter

In the body of the letter state your business as briefly and concisely as possible. There is no need to use more formal English than you would use when talking to someone who is in the room with you. For example, don't write, "In re your letter of April 6 . . ." Instead say, "Regarding your letter of April 6 . . ."

It's also important to resist the urge to recount your complaint or compliment in too much detail. A business letter that runs longer than one page isn't nearly as effective as one that's short and to the point.

The Closing

An appropriate closing to any business letter is "Sincerely" or "Regards."

TITLES

Even though we rarely use them in conversation anymore—or perhaps because we don't use them—titles cause a lot of problems when people write formal or business letters. As a general rule it's better to err on the side of respect in correspondence. Elderly people and public officials should be addressed as "Mr." or "Mrs." (or "Miss" or "Ms.") or whatever other title is appropriate.

Mrs. Miss, and Ms.

Many single and married women today prefer Ms., which has become popular for business and social purposes. It solves a lot of problems, not least of which is to give women one easy title that is the equivalent of Mr.

If a married woman uses Ms., it is often a tip-off that she also continues to use her own name. In practice, Mrs. is almost always adopted by women who use their husband's surnames. Ms. (pronounced "Miz"), however, is appropriately used with a woman's own surname or her husband's surname.

Those who still prefer the now somewhat old-fashioned Miss may continue to use it when addressing single women. A married woman, though, who states her preference to be addressed as Ms. should be. I have a friend whose mother persists in addressing her by her "married name" even though my friend has never adopted her husband's name. The mother undoubtedly thinks she is making a point, but in fact she is confusing the situation by refusing to address her daughter by the name she actually uses.

Jr., Sr., II, III

Some families customarily name children after living relatives. The son of Charles Harvey Johnson, for example, may also be named Charles Harvey Johnson. In the case of men, this has led to several special designations that help us tell father apart from son (or nephew or grandfather).

Generally, when a son is given his father's exact name, "Jr." is appended to his name. When a man is named after an uncle or grandfather or some other relative, a numerical designation ("II" or "III") is used, although in some families this applies as well to a son who is named after his father.

When a father dies, his son usually, after an appropriate amount of time, drops the Jr. from his name. However, if his mother is still living and is likely to be confused with his wife, he may retain Jr. as long as his mother lives.

Unlike Jr. and Sr., numerical designations are not usually dropped. Few families, though, extend them beyond III or IV. If a name is changed even slightly—say, if Charles Harvey Johnson's nephew is named Charles Wilson Johnson—there is no need for a numerical designation.

Even though women share family names, there have never been any formal designations to differentiate them, perhaps because for many years women took their husband's name when they married and thus set themselves apart.

Doctors

In our society the title "Doctor" is bestowed on physicians and on academicians who have earned their doctorate degrees. But only physicians use their title socially, and even this custom is on the wane. Professors use their title in the classroom—or in academic circles.

Physicians who do use their titles socially would expect them to appear on invitations and in other correspondence. Thus invitations to a married female physician would be addressed to "Mr. and Dr. E. G. Jones" and correspondence to two physicians would read "Dr. and Dr. John Smiley" or "Drs. Mary and John Smiley."

Lawyers

Some lawyers (both male and female) use the title "Esq." (for Esquire) after their names, especially on stationery and in formal correspondence. The title is optional, though, and many lawyers do not bother with it.

Titles of Government Officials

The following chart shows how to address public officials in writing and in conversation.

Person	Address for Letter	Letter Greeting	Speaking To
The President	The President The White House Washington, D.C.	Dear Mr. President	Mr. President, first time; thereafter, sir
The First Lady	Mrs. Adams A joint envelope would read The President and Mrs. Adams	Dear Mrs. Adams	Mrs. Adams
The Vice President	The Vice President The White House	Dear Mr. Vice President	Mr. Vice President, initially; thereafter, sir
Vice President's Wife	Mrs. John Smythe	Dear Mrs. Smythe	Mrs. Smythe

Person	Address for Letter	Letter Greeting	Speaking To
Speaker of the House	The Honorable George Jackson Speaker of the House	Dear Mr. Speaker	Mr. Speaker
Chief Justice of the Supreme Court	The Chief Justice The Supreme Court	Dear Mr. Chief Justice	Mr. Chief Justice
Justices of the Supreme Court	Justice William Johnson The Supreme Court	Dear Mr. Justice	Justice Johnson
Cabinet Members	The Honorable James Elliott	Dear Mr. Secretary	Mr. Secretary or Secretary Elliott
Attorney General	The Honorable Jane Talley	Dear Ms. Attorney General	Ms. Attorney General
Senator	The Honorable Edward Dailey United States Senate	Dear Senator Dailey	Senator or Senator Dailey
Representative	The Honorable Jean Wicks	Dear Ms. Wicks	Ms. Wicks
Governor	The Honorable Sarah Andrew Governor of Illinois	Dear Governor Andrew	Governor or Governor Andrew
Mayor	The Honorable Evan Hunt	Dear Mayor Hunt	Mayor Hunt

Military Titles

The military adheres strictly to the use of titles, and retired military personnel often continue to be called by their titles, especially if they reached a high rank.

The chain of command for army, air force, and marine corps titles is as follows:

- General
- Major General
- Brigadier General
- Colonel
- Lieutenant Colonel
- Major
- Captain
- First Lieutenant
- Second Lieutenant

Titles for the navy and coast guard are as follows:

- Admiral
- Vice Admiral
- Rear Admiral
- Captain
- Commander
- Lieutenant Commander
- Lieutenant
- Lieutenant, junior grade
- Ensign

Air force, army, and marine corps officers of all grades are addressed in writing and in conversation by their rank and their name. Naval officers above lieutenant commander are addressed by their rank and name; below this rank they are addressed as Mr. or Ms. or Miss (never Mrs.) but are introduced by their rank. In all branches, double-worded titles are generally abbreviated in speaking to one word: lieutenant commander becomes commander, for example, and lieutenant, junior grade, becomes lieutenant.

Person	Address for Letter	Letter Greeting	Speaking To
Commissioned Officer	Lieutenant Drexler, USMC *or* Lieutenant Colonel Jasmine Day, USN	Dear Lieutenant Drexler *or* Dear Colonel Day	Lieutenant Drexler *or* Colonel Day
Warrant Officers (these technically fall between commissioned and non-commissioned officers)	Chief Warrant Officer Marie Chapell, USMC	Dear Chief Warrant Officer	Chief Warrant Officer *or* Ms. Chapell
Non-commissioned Officers	Sergeant Will Brown	Dear Sergeant Brown	Sergeant Brown
Chaplains	Chaplain Dee Willow	Dear Chaplain Willow	Chaplain Willow (Catholic chaplains are often called "Father" and Jewish clergy are called "Rabbi")

Clergy Titles

The clergy also use titles, which are sometimes retained after retirement as a gesture of respect.

Person	Address for Letter	Letter Greeting	Speaking To
Protestant Minister with Doctorate	The Reverend Dr. Addison Wiley	Dear Dr. Wiley	Dr. Wiley
Without Doctorate	The Reverend Sam Wilcox	Dear Reverend Wilcox	Rev. Wilcox (never Reverend without a name)
Protestant Episcopal Bishop	The Right Reverend Sandra Mason, Presiding Bishop	Dear Bishop Mason	Bishop Mason
Rabbi	Rabbi Abraham Cohen	Dear Rabbi Cohen	Rabbi Cohen, *or* Rabbi
The Pope	His Holiness John Paul II *or* His Holiness the Pope	Your Holiness	His Holiness, The Pope
Cardinal	His Eminence Francis Cardinal Anderson	Your Eminence	His Eminence, Cardinal Anderson

Person	Address for Letter	Letter Greeting	Speaking To
Archbishop and Bishop, Roman Catholic	The Most Reverend James Connor	Your Excellency	The Archbishop of (diocese)
Monsignor	The Right Reverend James Riley	Dear Monsignor James Riley	Monsignor Riley
Priest	The Reverend Henry Johnson, *followed by the initials of his order*	Dear Reverend Father *or* Dear Father Johnson	Father Johnson
Member of a Religious Order	Brother John, *followed by the initials of his order*	Dear Brother John	Brother John
	Sister Juanita, *followed by the initials of her order*	Dear Sister Juanita	Sister Juanita

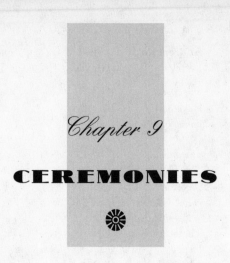

Chapter 9

CEREMONIES

Despite a steady trend toward less formal living that has lasted for several decades, most of us still appreciate a little ceremony in our lives—and some of us like a lot of it. Ceremonies—the formal and informal rituals that shape our lives—have a definite purpose, and that is to give us a sense of rootedness in our world.

Announcing the New Baby's Arrival

Ceremony surrounds us from the moment of birth. We send birth announcements to tell others the news of the new arrival, and we have certain religious ceremonies that welcome babies into the world.

Birth Announcements

The first news of a new arrival is by word of mouth. Parents are so excited that they call everyone they know to share the joyous news. But within a few weeks of a baby's birth, most parents like to send printed announcements as well. Birth announcements can be either formal or informal. Both are acceptable, and what you send depends entirely on your personal preference.

Formal announcements, which are making a comeback after several years' absence, consist of two cards joined with a ribbon—pink for girls, blue for boys, and yellow or green for those who wish to be less gender oriented. The large card contains the parents' name and address, and the small card gives the baby's name and birth date.

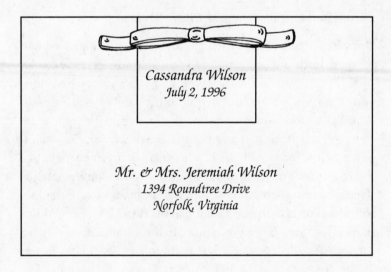

Cassandra Wilson
July 2, 1996

Mr. & Mrs. Jeremiah Wilson
1394 Roundtree Drive
Norfolk, Virginia

FORMAL BIRTH ANNOUNCEMENT

The obvious disadvantage of this card is that it doesn't contain the baby's weight and other vital statistics that so many people like to include. You could add a line or two about this, since formal birth announcements do not really have to follow any set format (they aren't "formal" in any significant sense; this is just the term used to describe them). What you add is limited more by space than anything else.

Informal announcements come in two varieties: custom printed and preprinted. Custom-printed announcements are ordered from stationery stores or jewelers. Preprinted announcements are purchased in stationery stores and card shops. There is great variety even in the preprinted announcements, enough to please everyone's taste.

One last trend in birth announcements, which I applaud, is to include older siblings' names along with the parents'. I think this makes the siblings feel included at a time when they are likely to be feeling a little left out.

Birth Announcement from a Single Woman

I'm often asked whether it's appropriate for a single woman to send birth announcements—and the answer is yes. The birth of a baby is always a joyous and newsworthy occasion, and I see no reason not to announce every new arrival. Another time a woman may send a birth announcement by herself is when mother and father have divorced or separated prior to the baby's birth. If a woman is divorced or separated, it does not make sense to issue a joint announcement. The announcement comes from her alone, based on the fact that she is usually the custodial parent. If she has changed her name, she uses her new name. In other words, she is no longer Mrs. George Perez but will probably be Maria Perez. If she has returned to her maiden name; this is what she should use.

Divorced and separated fathers may also send announcements (although usually only the custodial parent does this). But when both parents are sending announcements, they must divide their list so none of their friends and relatives receive two. That would be tacky and rivalrous. Except for the fact that one parent's name is missing, the birth announcement issued by a single parent reads like any other birth announcement.

When a single woman is living with the father of her child, and they have a long established relationship, they may send joint announcements.

Birth Announcements from a Same-Sex Couple

When a same-sex couple either has or adopts a child, they will of course want to send a birth announcement. Both their names will appear on the announcement.

Adoption Announcements

The arrival of an adopted child is as joyous an occasion as the birth of a new baby, and announcements should definitely be sent. They should, however, clearly be adoption announcements, not birth announcements. Unfortunately there are few preprinted announcements for adopted children, but specially printed ones seem to work better because the information you will want to include is unique. Obviously you'll want to say that the new family member is adopted, and you may want to include the child's age, especially if the child is not a newborn. I recently received a heartwarming card announcing the adoption of a Chinese girl, and it included the line "Arrived from China, June 6, 1995." It pleased me because it showed so much pride in the child's background.

The usual wording of an adoption announcement is as follows:

MR. AND MRS. WILLIAM QUENTIN

ARE PLEASED TO ANNOUNCE

THE ADOPTION OF THEIR SON

WILLIAM LEE

MARCH TENTH, 1996

AGE, EIGHT MONTHS

A single person adopting a child sends the same kind of announcement but uses only his name. On formally worded announcements, titles (Mr., Miss, or Ms.) are used. On less formal announcements, you may prefer to drop the title.

NAMING A CHILD

Obviously, to send a birth announcement, you must have already selected a name for your child. Many people like to choose a name with some special significance. For decades this meant a biblical name, but these have lost out today to more ecumenical names.

Many people honor family members by naming children after relatives. Among some groups, the firstborn son or, occasionally, a later one (or all your sons, if you happen to be George Foreman) is named after his father. Either Jr. or the Roman numerals (I, II) are used to distinguish father from son. (See page 221 for more on this subject.) Girls are occasionally named after their mothers, especially in the South, but when a girl is given her mother's name, these designations are not added to her name.

Under canonical law, Roman Catholics are expected to give their children a saint's name as a first or middle name.

Jewish families often name their children for deceased relatives, but rarely for living relatives. In addition, a Jewish child who is named for someone typically does not carry the same exact name, as is the Christian practice, but instead has a different name with the same first initial. Jewish children are also given a Hebrew name.

Things to Think about When Naming a Child

The only other considerations in naming a child are to settle on something that won't embarrass or be too awkward for him. A first name that does not match, or at least complement, the child's last name, for example, can create problems.

Consider how a first and last name go together. If you have a very long last name, you may want to give your child a simple first name. And the reverse is also true: If your last is Smith or Jones, you may want to add a little balance by giving your child a first name that has a bit of heft.

Names that are puns or attempts at humor should be avoided. We've all heard what I hope are apocryphal stories about people named Ima Hogg and Flora Fana, but I hope that none of us actually do this to our children.

Consider, too, in selecting your child's name what nicknames will be—or could be—derived from it. Many names have a diminutive. William becomes Bill or Billy, and Suzanne becomes Sue or Susie. If you like diminutives, that's fine, but if you don't like them, then you should choose a name that doesn't lend itself to nicknames.

Finally, in choosing a name, parents should also consider a child's monogram. Although monograms are not much used these days, they will undoubtedly come back in style at some point, and you won't want your child to be stuck with something silly, such as HOG or TAD. It's safest all around, in fact, to avoid a monogram that spells anything at all.

RELIGIOUS CEREMONIES SURROUNDING BIRTH

Most religions have some sort of ceremony to welcome a newborn into their community. Christians baptize their children. Jewish boys are circumcised at a ceremony called a bris, and Jewish girls are recognized at a naming ceremony.

Baptism

Many religions practice infant baptism, and when they do, the baptism is usually accompanied by a small ceremony and a party afterward to celebrate.

Baptisms are held sometimes in church, sometimes at home. The choice depends upon your religion, your clergyperson's preference, and your own desires. The party afterward is usually held at the home of the new parents, although there may be a communal celebration at church as well. If the baptism is held in a church, anyone may attend, and the ceremony is usually part of the weekly service.

In either instance, invitations, either telephoned or written, are sent to family members who would not ordinarily attend the service, asking them to join you. These should note whether there is a party afterward and should also give the particulars, such as time and place.

An invitation to a baptism might read as follows:

> Dear June,
>   We are christening little Susie on Sunday, June 8, at 10 a.m. at the Christ Memorial Church, which is located at 322 Oak Street. Afterward, we're having a brunch at our house. I hope you'll be able to join us for this special day.
>
> Love,
> Jeannette

Family members and close friends are among those invited to a baptism. Work colleagues and acquaintances are not usually asked to such an intimate party.

Partly out of custom, partly because it is part of a religious service, and partly because mother and baby usually are in better form, christenings are held in the morning, with a party following immediately afterward. The party is a breakfast, a brunch, or a lunch. A white cake is traditionally served for dessert, and baby is often toasted with champagne, as well.

Godparents

Godparents are not chosen in every religion, but where they are, their role usually is to sponsor the child at baptism and more officially to oversee the child's religious education. A godparent is also a special friend to the child, a member of the child's extended family. Most religions prefer that godparents be of the child's faith, and a few require this; but among Protestants, denominational differences do not matter when choosing godparents. During the ceremony, godparents usually hold the child at least briefly, and at the party afterward, they offer a toast to the baby's health and well-being.

Gifts

Babies are generally given gifts at a christening. Those in the immediate family—grandparents, godparents, aunts and uncles, siblings—may choose to give a special baptism present even if they have already given a baby present.

Traditional baptism presents include a white Bible or prayer book, baby jewelry, or a silver baby gift, such as a cup or mug, bowl, or spoon—in other words, something the child will carry through life and always associate with her first important ceremony. Jewelers and specialty gift stores carry baby jewelry, which consist of small lockets, rings, and (these days) pierced earrings. Either gold or silver is acceptable.

If you have not gotten a baby gift yet, a baptism is a nice time to do so. If you have already given a gift, and especially if it was a generous one, then it is not necessary to bring another if the baptism occurs soon after birth. If you don't want to arrive empty-handed, you may bring a small token, such as white booties or a hat.

Christening Gowns

What a baby wears at its baptism depends upon the parents' taste and preference. Traditionally the baby is dressed in white, although pastel colors are acceptable as well.

The traditional baptismal dress, whether for a boy or a girl, is a long white, often elaborately lace-trimmed and be-ribboned gown, usually of cotton but sometimes of another fabric as well. Some families have lovely christening gowns that have been handed down from one generation to the next, while others buy new ones. If you want to dispense with this, then the baby should be dressed in his best white or pastel outfit.

What Everyone Else Wears

Parents should wear whatever they would wear to church, keeping in mind that they will stand up in front of the congregation during the baptismal ceremony. Virtually no church requires women to wear hats, but a mother may want to do this to complete her outfit or may otherwise want to dress a bit more formally than usual. Men should wear dark suits. Guests attending the baptism and party afterward should also wear clothes appropriate for a church ceremony or any other slightly dressy party.

When There Is No Baptism

Many parents today choose not to baptize their infants. If this is right for you, you might still consider having a party to welcome the new arrival. A party like this can incorporate aspects of the christening such as the white cake and the champagne toasts. Some parents even use this occasion to dress an infant in the family's ceremonial christening dress.

Bris/Naming Ceremony

Jewish people celebrate the arrival of a new baby with either a bris (for a boy) or a naming ceremony (for a girl).

Unless there is a health reason, a bris takes place on the eighth day of the child's life. A *moyel* (someone who specializes in performing this ceremony) or a physician can perform the circumcision, which is usually done at home. A bris is held in the morning, and a brunch is served afterward. Most people will not have seen the baby yet, so baby presents are often brought to the ceremony.

Traditionally invitations are not issued for a bris; people simply know that they should go. But in these busy days it is undoubtedly safer to phone invitations or to issue them when you call people about the birth. Written invitations are not sent, for the simple reason that there is no time to prepare them.

Mother and infant may not be too much of a presence at a bris since both are still recuperating from the birth, and the baby may be stressed from the circumcision as well. Mothers are usually advised to nurse their babies for a while after the bris, but whether the mother is nursing or simply resting, she should not be disturbed unnecessarily. This is one of those occasions where the hostess is exempt from her usual duties if she doesn't feel up to them.

A naming ceremony (the Jewish welcoming ceremony for a girl) is held within a few weeks of birth during a regular religious service in a temple or synagogue. In these days of egalitarianism, many parents are choosing to hold a small party afterward, but often there is not one. Alternatively, after the ceremony the parents may sponsor a kiddush—that is, a small breakfast for the entire congregation—at the temple or synagogue. As with a bris, invitations are telephoned.

Dress for Baby and Guests
No special clothing is worn by the baby for a bris or a naming ceremony. Guests should dress as they would for any other religious service.

Gifts
Although gifts are given, they are usually not ceremonial like baptismal gifts. Typical baby gifts—clothing, equipment, stuffed animals, and toys—as well as gifts of money or stocks and bonds are generally given.

First Communion

This is a ceremony held in the Catholic Church when children are six or seven years old. Like a christening, the first communion is followed by a breakfast, brunch, or lunch attended by family and close friends. A white cake is usual as dessert. Invitations may be written or telephoned, whichever you prefer.

Dress
In some communities girls wear white, rather formal dresses and elaborate veils. If this kind of dress is not called for, then girls usually wear white dresses suitable for church. Boys wear dark suits or white shirts with dark pants, whichever is

required. Guests should dress as they would for any religious service.

Gifts

Traditionally ceremonial presents, such as a Bible or prayer book, religious or other jewelry, or a small piece of silver, are given at a first communion. Frivolous presents are not considered appropriate.

Christian Confirmation

At age thirteen, many Protestants formally join their church, usually after taking a special course of religious instruction. Family and friends are invited to attend the service and also to a celebration afterward.

Like a christening, the confirmation is usually celebrated with a breakfast, brunch, or lunch held either at a restaurant or at home. Typically this is a family gathering, although a few friends may be included, especially if they are close to the child.

Invitations

Invitations are usually extended informally, often by telephone, sometimes by personal, handwritten note, and less often by preprinted invitation. Written invitations are usually called for only if a large party is planned. Children should be permitted to invite several friends to help them celebrate this special occasion.

Dress

Boys and girls dress conservatively for their confirmation. Girls wear modest white or pastel dresses or suits, and boys wear dark suits and ties. A confirmation is still sometimes the occasion for a girl's first pair of high-heeled shoes and nylon hose or her first "grown-up" dress. Black is never appropriate for a confirmation. Mothers wear pretty dresses or suits, whatever they usually wear to church services. Fathers wear dark suits. Guests dress in a similar manner.

Gifts

For a Christian confirmation, gifts are typically given, especially by parents, grandparents, and others who are close to the person being confirmed. At a Roman Catholic confirmation, the gifts are usually religious in nature—a Bible engraved with the recipient's name, a prayer book, a gold cross or a religious medal or charm. A Bible is an acceptable gift for Protestants as well, as is jewelry (religious or nonreligious depending upon the recipient's taste), a book, or stocks or bonds. A small piece of silver, such as a pen, a letter opener, or a box, is also traditional.

Jewish Confirmation/Bar or Bat Mitzvah

At age thirteen, a Jewish child is usually either confirmed or bar or bat mitzvahed, depending upon the congregation. Young people work very hard to prepare for this ceremony. They study Judaism, learn Hebrew, and prepare to read from the Torah for the first time. In addition, each child gives a small speech interpreting his or her Torah passage. After all the hard work, it's hardly surprising that the reward is a big party.

Immediately after the service, parents sponsor a kiddush at the synagogue. Then the family and friends usually repair to the parents' home, a restaurant, a hotel, or banquet hall, for a larger party that typically includes a sit-down dinner and dancing. Depending upon the parents' and the child's preference, a bar or bat mitzvah celebration can range from a modest home party to a large semiformal event held in a restaurant or banquet hall.

A bar mitzvah celebration can be akin to a wedding in terms of formality, entertainment, and expense and because of this has often been of more interest to the adults than to the children. In recent years, though, there has been a trend toward planning parties that appeal to the youngsters more than the adults. This usually means more casual dress, themes, food, and music.

Invitations

In keeping with the level of formality, invitations to the party range from handwritten notes to the elaborate, custom-printed variety. No one has to be invited to the post-service kiddush since immediately after the service the entire congregation convenes for this. Written or printed invitations should indicate the time of the service, usually around 10 A.M., as well as the time of the party, which often is not held until later that same day, most typically after the Sabbath has ended. (Customs vary with different communities, and some parties are held on the afternoon of the bar or bat mitzvah.)

The guest list for a bar or bat mitzvah can run into the hundreds. Family, of course, are included (these are first and foremost family events), as are close friends. Beyond this, many people also invite acquaintances, neighbors, and business colleagues.

In addition, the child should invite some friends. The issue of whether to invite all or part of a child's class always arises, just as it does with birthday parties. To this I can only say that if possible, and if affordable, it is always better to include as many as possible.

Dress

Boys wear dark suits to the ceremony, and girls wear special-occasion (albeit conservative) dresses. Girls often change into party dresses for the celebration held afterward, and boys may wear black tie if this is what the other men are wearing. A bat mitzvah girl at a more formal evening party should wear a dress appropriate to her age—slightly more grown-up, but not overly sophisticated, given the event.

Guests wear whatever they would to any other religious service; parents may opt for something a little nicer than usual since they will be standing on the *bimah* with their child. Depending upon the congregation, women may need to wear hats or other head coverings.

If the party afterward is not dressy, then parents and guests do not need to change clothes. But if it is held later at night and is more formal, then women usually change into short cocktail clothes and men wear dark suits, if not black tie. Obviously even more elaborate clothes may be worn, including long dresses, if the occasion calls for it.

Gifts

As is the case with weddings, anyone receiving a bar mitzvah invitation is obligated to send a gift. In addition, gifts, at least in some parts of the country, are almost as substantial as wedding gifts. Money, stocks, and bonds make popular gifts, as do reference books, books on Jewish history and culture, wallets and other small leather goods, jewelry, and electronic equipment—usually of a musical nature!

The size of the gift depends only on the closeness of the relationship. This means that if you are a relative or intimate family friend, you will give a larger gift than if you are a business colleague or an acquaintance.

Graduations

Although children start "graduating" these days as early as kindergarten, only two important graduations—high school and college—can be considered ceremonial enough to call for a special celebration.

Invitations

Invitations are always a problem at high school graduations because seats are in such short supply in most community high schools. Sometimes this is the case with college graduations as well. Many schools can give a student only four or six seats to the ceremony itself, and these are usually taken up by parents, siblings, and grandparents.

Many more invitations can be sent out for the party that follows the ceremony. Depending upon the affair's size and degree of formality, either a telephoned, handwritten, or preprinted invitation may be issued.

Invitations can go to both family and friends. Usually they do not go to acquaintances and business colleagues, except for those you see socially. They should also go to anyone who has played a special role in a child's life, including those who live out of town and may not be able to attend.

At one graduation I attended recently, for example, the mother had sent an invitation to an old friend who had given her daughter a handmade quilt as a baby gift. The two had remained close via letters over the years, and the mother thought the woman might enjoy the invitation just as a memento. But the friend was so delighted to be asked that she made plans to travel 1,200 miles to attend the party and brought another handmade quilt as a present. Reunions like this are priceless, and it is for this reason that you should err on the side of sentimentality when considering whom to invite.

Another mother I know used the occasion of her son's graduation to renew her friendship with his godmother. The two women had lost touch with each other years earlier, and although the godmother lived in a distant city and could not attend the graduation, she was thrilled with the invitation and arranged to visit her godson later that summer.

Finally, although it would be nice to invite the new graduate's friends, they often are not available since they are busy attending their own graduations.

Party

Graduation parties can be small or large, formal or informal. However, because they are held in the spring and early summer, they tend to be informal and are perfect for picnics, barbecues, and pool parties.

Gifts

You are not obliged to send a gift upon receipt of a graduation invitation, but many people do. Suitable presents are jewelry and small leather goods, luggage, sports equipment, electronic equipment and games, small appliances such as radios or compact disc players, or anything of a (relatively) permanent or lasting nature. Clothes usually are not given on this occasion, but there is no reason they could not be.

WEDDINGS

Weddings are one of the most important—and highly ceremonial—events in most people's lives. Entire books have been written about how to organize them, so this one will not dwell at length on the subject other than to provide enough information to get you started planning your special day. Of course, this section will also prepare you to be the perfect wedding guest. Before you begin to plan a wedding in any detail, you need to figure out what kind you want—or can afford—to have. Weddings basically come in three flavors: informal, semiformal, and formal. Which flavor you choose dictates the kind of invitations you will send, what you and the wedding party will wear, and the type of reception you will have.

The Formal Wedding and What It Entails

Formal weddings are often extravaganzas, very beautiful to participate in and lovely to attend. The bride and groom wear formal dress, which varies depending upon whether the wedding is held during the day or evening. For a bride this means a formal white or ivory dress, a long veil, and an even longer train. If the wedding is in the daytime, the dress will be only slightly more modest than if the big event is held at night.

For a daytime wedding, female guests wear short dressy dresses or suits, and men wear dark business suits with conservative shirts and ties. For a formal evening wedding, guests wear evening dress. If women wear long dresses, then men wear white tie; if women wear short cocktail dresses, then the men wear either black tie or a dark suit.

A formal wedding is usually followed by an elaborate, all-stops-out reception, which includes a cocktail hour, dinner, and after-dinner entertainment, usually in the form of dancing to a full orchestra or, at minimum, a band. Formal invitations are sent to this kind of wedding. For more about these, see page 209.

A formal wedding is the most expensive kind to have. It usually has the largest guest list, as well it should considering the pageantry involved. A guest list for a formal wedding is rarely under one hundred and may total three or four hundred people, although weddings with truly huge guest lists are rare except when public figures marry.

The Semiformal Wedding and What It Entails

At a semiformal wedding, the bride wears a long white dress, typically without a train, and a short veil or even no veil. Again, the dress will be more modest in the daytime than at night.

Female guests wear short street clothes, which get progressively dressier as the hour gets later. After 5 or 6 P.M. guests may wear very dressy clothes. Male guests wear dark suits, or black tie, if the wedding is held at night.

The reception for a semiformal wedding is often (but not always) more modest than that for a formal wedding. The food can range from a tea menu for an afternoon wedding, to a light or full buffet, to a sit-down dinner.

Often whether or not a meal is served has to do with familial and cultural expectations, as well as which part of the country one comes from. In large cities and in certain ethnic groups, it is expected that a meal will be served, and indeed it would be offensive if one were not. In the South and the Midwest, on the other hand, a tea menu is acceptable, particularly at an afternoon wedding. Music may be taped or live, although a full orchestra is rare—a small band or quartet are more the norm. Invitations are the same as for a formal wedding; for more information, see page 209.

A semiformal wedding can be as expensive as a formal wedding, or you can choose to spend less. You could opt for taped music, for example, or for a quartet of musicians rather than a band. Also, the guest list is smaller, usually anywhere from fifty to one hundred fifty people.

The Informal Wedding and What It Entails

At an informal daytime wedding, the bride wears a short dressy dress or suit, in white or a color, usually pastel. She may wear a hat with a short veil or no veil—or, for that matter, no hat at all if the presiding clergyperson has no objections. The groom wears a dark suit, usually gray or navy, a white shirt, and a conservative tie.

Female guests wear anything from dressy street clothes to cocktail dresses, if the hour is late. Male guests wear dark conservative suits or navy blazers with light-colored pants.

The reception differs little from that of a semiformal wedding. Anything from a simple reception to a sit-down meal is fine, and the music can be taped or live—or nonexistent. Information about invitations can be found in Chapter 8.

An informal wedding can be as large and expensive as a semiformal wedding or it can be a far simpler and less costly affair. The guest list can vary from just the immediate family members to about one hundred people.

Gifts

Wedding presents should be substantial, but you are never expected to give a gift that is beyond your means. They are usually domestic, and may be either practical or luxurious. Typical gifts include dishes, glassware, flatware, linens, appliances, even furniture. In some groups, it is the custom to give money, stocks or bonds.

Most couples register at one or more stores. One need not buy a wedding present that is listed on the bridal registry, but it does help to know what the couple would most like to receive.

Dress for Wedding Party

	Formal	Semiformal	Informal
Bride	Daytime: Long elaborate white dress in white or ivory, with train; long veil; gloves optional; simple jewelry.	Daytime: Long white dress; short veil; gloves optional; simple jewelry.	Daytime: Simple white or colored short dress or suit; simple jewelry; daytime hat if desired.
	Evening: Same, but dress is often less covered up; fabric more dressy.	Evening: Same, but dress can be less covered up; fabric more dressy.	Evening: Dressier short dress; cocktail dress; small cocktail hat.
Groom	Daytime: Gray cutaway coat with striped pants; gray vest; white dress shirt with turndown collar; gray-and-black-striped four-in-hand tie. Black socks and shoes; gray gloves optional.	Daytime: Black or charcoal sack coat; gray vest; white pleated shirt with turndown collar; black four-in-hand tie; black socks and shoes; gray gloves optional.	Daytime: Winter—dark suit; suit shirt; four-in-hand tie. Summer—white linen jacket; dark trousers; white suit shirt; four-in-hand tie; black socks and shoes.
	Evening: Black tail coat with matching pants; white vest; wing collar;	Evening: Winter—black tuxedo. Summer—white dress	Evening: Dark suit in winter or lighter suit in summer; white suit

Formal	Semiformal	Informal
white bow tie; white gloves; black silk socks; black dress shoes.	jacket with dark trousers; pleated shirt; cummerbund; black bow tie or conservative four-in-hand tie; black socks and shoes.	shirt; conservative four-in-hand tie; tuxedo if bride wears long dress.

	Formal	Semiformal	Informal
Mothers	Daytime: Short dressy dress or suit; hat and gloves optional.	Daytime: Dressy dress or suit; hat and gloves optional.	Daytime: Dress or suit suitable for religious service; hat and gloves optional.
	Evening: Long evening	Evening: Short dressy dress; cocktail dress.	Evening: Dressy dress or suit; possibly cocktail dress; hat and gloves optional.

Note: The father of the bride wears the same type of clothing as the groom and groomsmen, who all dress alike. The father of the groom may dress as if he is a member of the wedding party or he may dress like a guest, whichever he prefers.

RELIGIOUS SERVICES

Many of life's ceremonies and rituals center around religious services, and these days we often find ourselves at other people's religious services. However, it is not always easy or comfortable to be a guest at a religious ceremony that is unfamiliar to us. We want to do what's right, but aren't always sure what that is. Fortunately there are some guidelines to help us get through these situations. They are designed both to honor those who practice a different religion and not to impinge on our own religious beliefs.

Protestant Services

Dress varies greatly with the congregation, but women will always be comfortable in a conservative dress, just as men will be comfortable in a conservative suit. Hats are not required for either sex. As a gesture of respect, men remove their hats upon entering a Protestant house of worship.

During the service, stand when others stand and sit when they sit. Hymns and prayers are often sung and spoken communally. Protestants bow their heads to pray, but people who aren't comfortable doing this need not do so. Similarly, you need not recite any prayer that would make you uncomfortable.

In most Protestant churches all are welcome to take communion when it is offered, but those of other faiths often do not wish to participate.

Roman Catholic and Eastern Orthodox Services

Conservative dress for men and women is always appropriate regardless of what other parishioners are wearing. People often go casually dressed to regular mass, and if someone asks you to go and indicates that your dress, even if casual, is appropriate, then it is.

Hats, which used to be required of women, are still worn on formal occasions and are never out of place. A scarf may be substituted. As a gesture of respect, male lay parishioners remove their hats upon entering the sanctuary.

Catholics stand and kneel during services. Visitors should stand when the congregation stands, but they may remain sitting when congregants kneel if they wish.

Communion in the Catholic or Eastern Orthodox churches is reserved for members. Simply stay in your seat when the parishioners go forward to receive it.

Jewish Services

Conservative dress is mandated in some synagogues and is simply the custom in others. Women usually do not attend services bare armed, and they wear hats or some head covering in all Orthodox and at some Conservative and Reform services. Men's heads are covered as a sign of respect, and they may wear prayer shawls as well. Visitors also may be asked to wear yarmulkes and prayer shawls; if so, these will be provided at the front of the sanctuary. Men and women will sit separately in a very Orthodox synagogue.

Jews do not kneel to pray, nor do they bow in the same way that Christians do. Instead they *daven*, a weaving, fluid, bowing motion. If you are a non-Jewish guest, you will not do this, but you should stand respectfully when others are praying. Also, Jewish congregants tend to pray more individually than do Protestants and Catholics. As individuals finish a prayer, they sit down. You should stand at the start of prayers like this and you may sit as soon as others begin to sit. Everyone stands when the doors to the chamber holding the Torah are opened and remains standing as a sign of respect as long as they are open. Guests should follow this custom.

There is more movement in a Jewish service than in either a Protestant or a Catholic service. Congregants will walk to the *bimah,* or altar, to participate in the service. Upon returning to their seats, they are often congratulated by other people, who stand to shake their hands and offer a comment or two.

Muslims

By the end of the century there will be more people of the Muslim faith than of the Jewish faith in the United States. Many are and will continue to be conservative in their religious practices. As we mix more, we will learn more about one another's ways, but for the present here are some helpful hints.

Shoes are never worn in a mosque. Slip them off when you arrive and reclaim them on departure. You need not pray, but you should maintain a respectful expression and posture while others do. Speak quietly. Dress conservatively (long sleeves and pants or skirts) when visiting a mosque.

Muslims stop what they are doing to pray to Allah five times a day. Non-Muslims do not participate even when visiting in a Muslim country, but it is rude to show any signs of irritation or to in any way interrupt the prayers.

Ramadan is a major holiday, one month long, during which adult Muslims fast during the day and gather for a large feast each night. If you know it is Ramadan, it is appropriate to mention this and even to extend your good wishes. Muslims may not accept invitations or otherwise socialize during this holiday.

Muslim women, like ultrareligious Jewish women, often dress conservatively. This usually involves long skirts and sleeves, as well as head coverings. It is never polite to ask about this dress or to comment on it. In many parts of the world it is improper to touch a woman, even to shake her hand. Until you know someone, therefore, it is better to err on the side of conservatism.

———

NOT ALL CEREMONIES ARE AS EXPANSIVE AS THE ONES DE-scribed here. Many families have their own private customs and ceremonies, special moments they share with one another. Whether your ceremonies are public or private, I encourage you to maintain them with care. They perform an important function in our lives, which is to anchor us to our time and place in the world.

Chapter 10

LOSSES

MOST PEOPLE APPRECIATE AND ARE COMFORTED BY THE ceremonies and rituals that surround death when they lose someone they love, but few of us think about these rituals until we need to. Then we scramble to figure out what has to be done and what we want to do. This chapter covers the basic rituals and ceremonies that surround life's saddest moments. Reading it now will help you be prepared later.

WHAT TO DO FIRST

When someone dies, the first step is to call a funeral director and a clergyperson. If you don't know someone to call, ask for advice. The social worker at the hospital, if your loved one died there, can advise you, as can the hospital chaplain and friends and close relatives who are with you at the time. In addition, when you speak with a clergyperson or a funeral director, either can put you in touch with the other. You do not have to be a member of a congregation or even actively religious to seek help at such a time, although obviously you will call a clergyperson of your faith. The funeral director will also be someone who shares your religion.

Making Plans

Calling these two people will set in motion the funeral arrangements that need to be made. Both are trained to deal with those under stress and guide them through what must be done. By working with them, you will sort out what seem to be overwhelming details, such as where to hold the funeral or memorial service, whether you want flowers or donations to a charity, what music you prefer, what eulogies you would like, and what, if any, seating arrangements must be made.

You will also need to focus on the costs involved, and this is best done at an early stage. The funeral director will present a bill for his services, which will include the casket and any other services he supplies, and the clergyperson will expect a donation.

Notifying Family and Friends

The next step is to notify friends and family of the loss. The bereaved can do this personally or, as is more often the case, can ask friends to help out—or even to make most of the phone calls.

Today, most people learn of the death of a relative or friend via a telephone call. Even transcontinental calls are inexpensive, but if you decide this is not the best way to deliver the news to someone so far away, then it's acceptable to send a day letter or a telegram.

Even distant relatives and friends should be notified, and

in a timely enough fashion so they can attend the funeral or memorial service if they wish (or at least be aware that it is going on). Sometimes well-meaning friends and relatives decide to notify someone after the funeral of a loved one, especially when they feel the person would not be able to attend the service. This is generally not appropriate. Regardless of whether someone can attend a funeral, he or she deserves to know about the death as soon as possible.

Although it may be trickier to know which friends to notify right away, and trickier still if the deceased person was estranged from some people, the general rule is to notify everyone. A funeral presents a last opportunity to come to terms with someone with whom one has had a breach. It should be a time to suspend petty—and even large—quarrels and come together in a spirit of forgiveness. The bereaved should give everyone, family and friends, a chance to do this.

When a Family Member Is Not Told about a Death
The decision not to tell someone about the loss of a loved one is a serious one and should not be made lightly. Sometimes, however, not bringing sad news is the kind thing to do—as with someone who is very elderly and frail or terribly ill. Because this decision requires the collusion of many family members, it is best to discuss the situation and then decide together.

FUNERAL PREPARATIONS

Most families want to hold some kind of service, whether or not it is religious and whether it is actually a funeral or the increasingly common memorial service.

Who Makes the Decisions?

The decisions that must be made in the hours and days after a death are the responsibility of the next of kin. Spouses make decisions for one another. Siblings make decisions jointly about the death of a parent in the absence of a spouse, and parents make them about a child.

Sometimes there are problems for unmarried couples living together and for same-sex couples. Legally, in such situations and in the absence of a will, a family can take custody of the departed and plan any kind of funeral or burial they wish. They can, and have been known to, exclude the partner. This is most likely to happen if there are long-standing bad feelings between the parties. And unfortunately it happens at the very moment when everyone is most vulnerable.

Apart from the fact that you need to protect yourself with a will if you are in such a situation, there is also a kind—and yes, a polite—way to handle such a predicament. In the best of all possible worlds, the two parties would make the arrangements together, each honoring the other's customs, beliefs, and values as much as possible. But for those who cannot manage this, here is what is right: Honor the person's partner in the same way that you would honor a spouse. In effect, if your child or your parent has lived with someone and has maintained a long-standing relationship with that person, then the blood relatives should yield to the deceased's partner as if she or he were a spouse.

Even if for some reason the family makes the arrangements, the partner should be included—and again, honored, as a spouse would be. He or she should sit with the family, mourn with them, and be able to take comfort from them at this especially painful time. One also hopes the reverse would be true, that the family would derive comfort from the person who loved their relative.

Choosing the Casket

The casket is the primary expense of a funeral. On the day of death or the day after, two or more family members will go to the funeral home to settle on a casket. No one should ever be pressured into buying something he cannot afford, nor should a bereaved person hesitate to choose a plain casket over a more elaborate one. Some religions, such as Judaism, even require that the deceased be buried in a modest casket. But in other religions caskets are sometimes very elaborate and choosing a plain one would be considered an act of insensitivity.

Even though it will be a difficult time to think about money, you should be completely open about your desires and what you can spend, and a professional funeral director should abide by your wishes. There should be no pressure, only gentle suggestions and advice.

There are and will continue to be outlandish caskets—I read recently about a man who insisted on being buried in a favorite car. But the safest thing is to choose a traditional casket, not least because of the expense and legal entanglements that can accompany an untraditional choice.

Choosing the Burial Clothes

In the same vein, it's better to bury a loved one in conservative clothing. There are always exceptions—the woman who was buried in a favorite, and very revealing, negligee; the man who was buried in a favorite tie-dyed T-shirt from the sixties—but as with very unusual wedding clothes, there is something undignified about such garments, especially on a deceased person.

Most people are buried in clothes that would be appropriate to wear to a religious service. For men this usually means a dark suit, a white or pastel shirt, and a tie. For women it means a dress or a suit. The colors are usually dark, but not necessarily black—nor need they be dark. While red or other very bright colors might not be appropriate, most other colors are—especially if the clothing in question happens to have been a favorite of the deceased.

Children are often buried in white, or at least in a white shirt or blouse. As with adults, something one might wear to a religious service is appropriate. In some Protestant faiths, adults are also buried in white. Orthodox Jews are often buried in a shroud, Conservative and Reform Jews in street clothes of the kind just described.

Jewelry is removed, although wedding bands are sometimes left on. This is a matter of personal preference, but friends and family should intervene gently if the next of kin seems inclined to bury someone wearing an expensive piece of jewelry.

Care of the Body

The body will be removed from the hospital or house by the funeral director, usually within hours of death. It goes to the funeral home and stays there until after the service, if the service is held in the funeral home, or until an hour or so before a church service. If makeup and hairdressing are required, the funeral director can make arrangements for this. Family members may visit if they choose to do so, although they should call first to be sure a visit is convenient, since several hours will be required for an autopsy or embalming.

Location for Service

Most Protestant and Jewish funerals take place in funeral homes; Catholic funerals are more often held in churches, after a wake at a funeral home.

PLANNING THE SERVICE

The service will be planned in conjunction with the clergyperson and the funeral director. A funeral generally lasts anywhere from thirty minutes to one hour. In a Roman Catholic or Eastern Orthodox service, if a full funeral mass is said, the service could last two hours or longer, especially if there are eulogies.

The clergyperson will open and close the service with special prayers and will also say a few words about the deceased if asked to do so. If no one else has been asked to speak, the clergyperson in effect gives the eulogy, but many families like to plan something more personal to honor a loved one. This may mean asking friends and colleagues to say a few words. It may mean reading a favorite poem or book passage of the deceased or any poem or passage that gives the family comfort. Often there is music as well, which may be either taped or live. A hymn may be sung, or part of a funeral requiem may be played. (Many funeral requiems require an hour or more to play in full, too long for most funerals.) Clergypeople can suggest appropriate readings and music, or the family can make their own choices. Usually (but not always) the music and readings are religious in tone.

A Word about Eulogies

A eulogy is a memorial speech or tribute that is given at a funeral or memorial service. As a general rule, the next of kin do not offer a eulogy, presumably because they are too bereaved to speak in public. They may ask others to do so, and anyone who considers herself close to the deceased may ask to say a word or two. Usually the family welcomes an offer to speak, and often, at the end of the formal part of the service, the clergyperson invites anyone who wishes to say something to stand and do so. If for any reason a family does not want someone to offer a eulogy, or does not want any eulogies, they may refuse the offer politely. There should be no hard feelings over a refusal, nor should any explanation be required.

Eulogies should be short and to the point. However well meant, meandering, vague speeches offer little comfort. I recently attended an incredibly uplifting funeral where nine people eulogized the man who had died. No one spoke more than five minutes. Each speaker told a revelatory anecdote and focused on a different aspect of the deceased's life—his writing, his teaching, his political activism. Mourners were left with a series of lovely emotional snapshots of their departed friend—images that would not soon fade.

NEWSPAPER NOTICES

Two other major items that must be taken care of right away are the death notice and the obituary. A death notice is a printed announcement that is purchased by the family to run in a newspaper. An obituary, in contrast, is an unpaid article that a newspaper chooses to run about the deceased. In large cities, obituaries are reserved for prominent citizens, while in small towns virtually anyone who dies may be newsworthy enough to warrant one.

Death announcements and obituaries run in the hometown newspapers of the person who has died, as well as in newspapers in other communities where she has lived and occasionally in the communities of the deceased's children as well. It is through the announcement that people learn of someone's death and find out when and where the funeral or memorial service will be held. For this reason, the announcement is always placed as soon as possible, with the aid of the funeral director. The obituary may run before or after a person's funeral.

The Announcement

The announcement contains the name, date of death, some reference to the cause of death (although the exact cause may not be mentioned, especially if the family prefers not to release this information), the names of immediate survivors, and the time, date, and place of the service. Also included may be a notice regarding flowers.

Survivors include the spouse and children (listed in chronological order from eldest to youngest), as well as parents and occasionally the siblings. In addition, most newspapers today—even the stodgy ones—have devised some means of listing a longtime partner who was not married to the deceased. His name should always be included, usually as a "longtime friend" or "companion."

A deceased woman's maiden name is given, as are the maiden names of survivors. Ages are not included unless they are needed for identification or unless the deceased was unusually young. In some local newspapers female survivors are traditionally listed before male ones, but in many other newspapers the reverse is true. The city or town where survivors currently reside is also sometimes included.

The time and place of the funeral or memorial service is described if they will be open to the public. Unless otherwise specified, a funeral is always considered public, and anyone may attend. Only when a notice says "Funeral private" is attendance by invitation only. In this case telephone calls to friends, acquaintances, and colleagues will serve as an invitation to the service.

Finally, there is usually a line or two about flowers and/or donations. Some people are comforted by flowers and welcome them; others prefer that the money be given to charity. If charitable contributions are requested, the charity is usually an organization associated with the deceased or with his cause of death.

Apart from the announcement the family puts in the paper, others connected with the deceased may take out announcements expressing their sympathy. These are purchased by colleagues and organizations or groups associated with the person who had died.

The Obituary

A family who wants an obituary as well as an announcement should notify the local newspapers. Many papers have a form that must be filled in. At other papers, family and friends write up the notice and submit it. In either instance, if there is going to be an obituary, a reporter from the newspaper will call to check the facts or make further inquiries.

FUNERAL FLOWERS/CHARITABLE
CONTRIBUTIONS

Flowers are sent to the funerals of Protestants and Catholics. Only one bouquet is permitted in the church during a Roman Catholic funeral; other flowers are left at the funeral home or transported to the cemetery.

If, in the death notice, the family requests that no flowers be sent, then only the closest family members may send them. Even then they should check with the next of kin, who may prefer that a spray or bouquet from the immediate family be the only tribute.

If no mention of either flowers or a charity is made in the death notice, then people decide individually what to do (and of course, sending flowers never precludes a contribution to charity as well). If a charitable contribution is made, the charity will send a notice, but these often come months after the death, so it is best to mention any donations in a condolence note. Finally, a charitable contribution never replaces a condolence note.

Flowers are never sent to the funerals of Orthodox or Conservative Jews and are rarely sent to the funerals of Reform Jews. If you want to comfort a friend or relative with flowers because they comfort you, you can always send or take them to the house during the shivah (see page 273) instead of the funeral. It is always appropriate to send a fruit basket to the home of Jewish mourners.

Addressing the Card

Funeral flowers are sent, literally, to the funeral, not to the family. In a small town the florist will know where to send them; in a large one you should have the address of the funeral home at hand when you place the order. Flowers are addressed "To the funeral of Mr. John Doe." The enclosed card reads "My [Our] deepest sympathy" or "With love and sympathy" or any other similarly appropriate message. Since the family members you are closest to may not be the ones to write the thank-you notes, it is necessary to sign your full name.

The Kinds of Flowers to Send

Funeral flowers are subdued. White is a traditional color, but pastel and autumnal flowers can also be sent. Red roses are not appropriate, nor is anything brightly colored. Certain varietals, such as gladiolus and chrysanthemum, have come to be associated with funerals, although they are used on other occasions as well. (In Europe, though, mums are so associated with funerals and mourning that they are inappropriate on other occasions.) In season, lilies, tulips, and even daisies are appropriate. A mixed bouquet is fine if it is subdued, as is a potted, even blooming, plant, such as a gloxinia, lily, or tulip.

Funeral flowers are sent in a vase or other container, including a basket, or they may be arranged in a spray. The large, often elaborate spray that covers the casket comes from the immediate family. As flowers arrive, ones from family members and very close friends are often moved closer to the casket than those from acquaintances and business associates.

Someone—either a family member or a close friend—should be asked to keep track of the flowers. A list describing each bouquet can be kept; alternately, the cards should be removed and a description of the flowers written on the back. Don't do this until right before the service, though, because people who pay condolence calls will want to see the flowers they have sent. Usually the person charged with the flower list goes to the funeral home an hour or so before the service to remove cards and/or draw up the list.

Finally, as much as flowers are appreciated at the funeral, it is also especially gracious—and sometimes an even greater kindness—to send a bouquet to a mourning person one or two weeks after the funeral. This is a way of letting a friend know that she is still in your thoughts—and it's a little boost of encouragement that may come when it is especially needed. This kind of bouquet can be colorful but should not be frivolous. A potted plant is a nice touch at such a time. The card can read simply "Love" or "Thinking of you."

Mass Cards

In lieu of flowers, many Catholics arrange for a mass to be said in a friend's or relative's memory. Call a church—yours or theirs—to make the arrangements (a donation is expected). A mass card is then sent to the family, and of course, you should mention this as well in the condolence note you send.

WHAT'S EXPECTED OF FAMILY AND FRIENDS

Upon hearing the news that a friend has died, family members and close friends usually gather at the home of the deceased or the next of kin. They come to offer their condolences, to help out with whatever must be done, and to bring food.

If the next of kin are not available when you call, don't ask to see them. They may need their time alone or may be in the midst of making plans. In either case, friends should not interfere but should simply offer their services and then do whatever is asked of them. In fact, it's better not to call when you first learn of a person's death, as the telephone is usually tied up for several hours while the family notifies people about the death.

There are two other functions friends may perform: They may be asked to serve as pallbearers, or (if they are especially close) they may give a eulogy.

Pallbearers and Ushers

Usually six pallbearers are chosen, but for ceremonial purposes as many as ten or twelve may be selected. Funeral directors prefer that pallbearers be honorary, but if the family wants their pallbearers to carry the casket, this can be arranged.

Professional pallbearers should be used when there might be a problem. If, for example, the deceased is so heavy that he could not be carried easily by friends, or if there aren't enough friends of about the same size to carry the casket, then it is best to use professional pallbearers. Ludicrous as this may seem, these things have to be taken into account even at such a time. A very short person and a very tall person simply cannot physically serve as pallbearers together.

When the pallbearers are honorary these problems are alleviated, since honorary pallbearers do not carry the casket, but instead walk beside or behind it. Another advantage to naming honorary pallbearers is that it more easily permits women to serve. Women have not traditionally been asked to be pallbearers, but there is no reason they could not be, especially if they are honorary.

In addition to pallbearers, ushers may be needed at a large funeral or memorial service. Their role is to greet people and help them find seats. Preferably they should know the deceased's family and friends, so they can steer close friends and family members to the front seats where they belong.

Members of the immediate family do not usually serve as pallbearers or ushers, although they may want to be on hand to greet people as they arrive. A son or daughter or sibling, for example, would not carry the casket, but grandchildren or nieces and nephews could perform this last task.

Calling Customs

Apart from close friends and family members who will automatically go to the home of the deceased upon learning the sad news, those who wish to pay their respects arrange to do so through a formal call.

An interval of three or four days, which is the formal mourning period, typically passes between the death and burial of a Protestant or a Catholic. During this period, friends and relatives pay condolence calls. The hours for calling are announced in the death notice.

Funeral Home Calls

For Catholics and Protestants, calls are typically made at the funeral home, less often at the home of the family. Upon arriving, callers are expected to sign the book that will be either outside or just inside the room containing the casket. Write your formal name and address, as the family will want to send you a thank-you note later.

Family members may or may not be present when you call. A funeral home call is made to pay your last respects to the deceased as much as it is to visit the family. If they are present, they may or may not rise to greet you, but when the opportunity presents itself, you should go to them to say hello and offer your sympathy. If you want to be sure to see family members, call during the times listed in the newspaper or call the funeral home to find out when they will be there.

Many people worry about what to say at such times, but nothing you can say is as important as your presence. Simply saying that you are sorry will suffice. If the family members and friends are reminiscing, as often happens at these events, you may feel free to join in.

If the casket is open, you may be asked if you would like to view the body, something that makes some people uncomfortable. But—and here's the important thing—no one need do this who does not want to. Usually a family member or friend will greet you when you arrive and ask if you would like to see the deceased. If you would, simply approach the casket, either by yourself or with a family member. Depending upon their faith, some people kneel, others cross themselves, and still others stand in contemplative silence. As is the case with a religious service, you need not do anything outside your usual religious practice. A Protestant, for example, does not cross himself, nor is a Protestant or a Jew expected to kneel.

If you are among those who prefer not to view an open casket, because of personal or religious preference, you need not approach the casket. If no one asks you, just don't go up to the casket. If someone does, simply say that you would prefer to remember the person as she was when you last saw her. One's feelings about these matters are intensely personal, and no one should ever feel the slightest bit awkward about declining to approach a casket.

THE FUNERAL

Family, friends, business colleagues, acquaintances—anyone who feels a tie to the deceased or his family—may attend the funeral if it is public.

Dress for funerals is conservative: dark suits and ties for men, suits or dresses for women. Wearing black is more a matter of personal preference these days than custom. Family members may wear black if they choose to, but even they need not. I once attended a funeral where the widow wore a lovely blue dress, a gesture that was all the more touching when she quietly explained that it was her husband's favorite. Bright colors are inappropriate on family members, and most other mourners will choose subdued clothes as well. Jewelry is subdued and often utilitarian.

Plan to arrive fifteen to thirty minutes before the service begins. Enter the funeral home or church quietly and sign the book that the funeral director has supplied. If there are ushers, wait to let them seat you. Unlike a wedding, here there is no discussion of whether you are a close friend or not. But if the ushers are themselves close friends, they will usually recognize other friends and relatives and seat them toward the front. Alternately, you may mention this fact.

Based on closeness to the deceased, mourners choose to sit nearer or farther from the front. Never take a seat in the far back unless the room is so full that you have no choice, because the family will be comforted by having people close to them during the service. The first few rows, however (and these are not always marked), are reserved for family members.

The casket is closed during a Catholic or Jewish service. It may be open for a Protestant service. Either way you may approach to pay your last respects, if you wish, before or after the service as you leave.

Jewish Funerals

A Jewish funeral takes place as soon as possible, on the day of death for an Orthodox Jew and the day after for a Conservative or Reform Jew. At a Jewish funeral the family may be receiving callers prior to the funeral at the funeral home. If so, someone will tell you where to go when you arrive. The funeral is followed by a formal period of mourning, a shivah, when the family receives callers in their home (see separate section on sitting shivah, page 273).

The Burial

Who attends a burial varies greatly depending upon the religion, the family's preference, and community customs. Unless the clergyperson announces that everyone is invited to the interment, it is usually private, and only family and a few close friends attend. However, in Judaism as many people as possible go to the burial to participate in the prayer service that is held at graveside.

Cremation

Cremation has become more prevalent in recent years. When someone is cremated, a funeral service may be held. There may or may not be a casket, depending upon the family's feelings. Sometimes in lieu of a casket there is an urn containing the ashes, and at other times there is no sign at all of the deceased. Apart from this, the service is the same—that is, the same prayers and eulogies may be given.

The Memorial Service

Today, many people choose to have a memorial service in place of, or in addition to, a funeral. In fact, the line between the two is becoming blurred.

For some people, one advantage to a memorial service is that it is less—or can be less—religious. There is still music,

somber if not nonsecular, and eulogies or other remem-
brances can be given by friends and family. In fact, many
memorial services today resemble nothing so much as organized wakes.

AFTER THE FUNERAL

After the burial, the family, and often other mourners as
well, usually gather for a breakfast or lunch. It may be held
in a home (even the home of the deceased), in a restaurant,
or in a room at the church or synagogue. The food is either
brought in by friends or catered, but the mourners do not
cook. A gathering like this is especially gracious and necessary if many people have come from out of town to attend
the funeral. It also gives family members, who may see one
another rarely, a chance to visit with one another.

The Wake

Sometimes the gathering after burial becomes a wake, although many people also consider the wake to be the period
between death and the funeral when friends and family call
at the funeral home. (In some parts of the country this is also
referred to as the viewing.) But in reality, a wake is more
like a contagious state of mind that can break out at almost
any time when people gather to mourn a loved one. It's
what happens when the reminiscing, at least among some
ethnic groups, turns into jokes and playful recall of the deceased's good—and bad—traits.

Some people find this kind of reminiscing a comfort—
and some do not. If you are among the former, stay and join
in because it can be a wonderful—and cathartic—way to say
good-bye to a friend. If you are not up for this, simply leave.

There is nothing wrong with either behavior, and everyone will understand.

Sitting Shivah

In the Jewish faith, the period of formal mourning that takes place after the funeral is known as "sitting shivah." Families sit shivah from three to seven days, with the exception of the Sabbath. An announcement is made of when and where the family will be sitting, but beyond this no formal invitations are extended.

People do not telephone in advance before paying a shivah call; they simply go. A call may be as brief as twenty minutes or as long as an hour; one's feelings must be the guide in this matter. Anyone who knew the deceased may pay a call. Families need all the support they can muster at such times, and no one whose life has been touched by the deceased or who is a friend of the mourners should feel too distant to call on them.

The door of the home of a family sitting shivah is open, and you simply walk in. Mourners may be sitting on boxes or small mourning chairs that have been provided for them, or they may sit on regular chairs. Food is provided, and it is polite to eat something. Very religious mourners will not shave during the week of mourning, and they may wear clothes that have been torn as a symbol of their mourning. At the end of the period of mourning, the rabbi will come to the house and help the mourners reemerge into the world.

When people arrive to pay a shivah call, the mourners may or may not rise to meet them. Mourners are not considered "hosts" even when sitting shivah in their own home, and they do not act this role. Mourners also will not be dressed up in any way, and those paying a shivah call can wear ordinary work clothes or even more casual dress.

There will be a table of food, especially if you call at mealtime, and you may help yourself. And if, like many people, you would rather not go empty-handed to a shivah call, either flowers, fruit, or a dessert is considered an appropriate offering. Don't present anything to the mourners, though. Instead take your gift to the kitchen or hand it to someone else (others will be around helping out). Finally, you need not be Jewish to pay a shivah call. Mourners welcome any show of support.

MOURNING THE LOSS OF A LOVED ONE

Whether someone has been ill for a long time or was taken suddenly, the death of a loved one is always one of life's severest blows, one that requires a period of mourning. There was a time when social custom dictated a long period of mourning—often as long as a year. During this interval, mourners' social lives were severely curtailed, and their distinctive dress announced their status to the world. In Victorian times mourning took place in carefully proscribed stages. A widow or widower wore black for several months, graduated to gray (or "demimourning," as it was known), and only slowly reemerged into a world of gay colors.

These specific customs have fallen by the wayside; in contemporary life, how long and how we go about doing our mourning are left up to us. Some bereaved people return to work within a week or so of losing a loved one, while others require more time to make even an initial recovery. During this period, friends want to help but often are unsure what to do.

The kindest thing you can do for a bereaved person is to let him mourn as long as he needs to while making it clear that you are available—in whatever form you are needed. Too often we try to force mourners into an active social life when what they really need is someone to ease them back into the world or even just to be with them while they mourn. If you really want to be kind to a friend in mourning, resist the urge to badger him to rejoin the world. Do call and offer your company on a walk or at a quiet dinner. Do include him in low-key family activities.

Only a very close friend who knows someone well should ever suggest that it is time to resume an active social schedule or to date again. The mourner will give a clue when she is ready for this.

STILLBIRTH AND MISCARRIAGE

A stillbirth or a miscarriage is among the most awkward social moments because we have no appropriate way to mourn either loss. Each tends to be played out privately and without the badly needed support of friends and family. Unfortunately, it seems, we must find our own way when our lives are touched by these sad events, but a few suggestions may help.

First, recognize the loss. Don't push it away. Express your own sorrow to your friends and family, and give them room to express theirs.

While religious services are not normally held for a stillbirth or a miscarriage, some people feel the need for some kind of remembrance. Your clergyperson may be able to assist you with a private service, or you may wish to hold your own. If it helps you mourn, you should by all means do this.

Watching a friend suffer through this kind of loss can be distressing, and it is hard to know what to say. Resist offering any evaluations of what has happened. Those who have experienced this kind of loss say they are not comforted by being told that they will have another child or that they lost the child because something was wrong with it.

Remember, people are always comforted by the simple words "I'm sorry." Offer your company if you can, and send a note or flowers if you like. Such gestures are greatly appreciated at these times. As with any loss, do not assume that your friends will be social right away; rather, give them time to mourn their loss, then wait for a cue from them that they are ready to be active again.

THE DEATH OF AN EX-SPOUSE

People often ask whether they can, or should, attend the funeral of an ex-spouse. The answer depends on several things, such as how long you have been divorced, what kind of relationship you have maintained, and most important, whether or not you have children together.

If you have children, they have lost a parent, and you will almost certainly want to help them mourn this loss. This may mean spending time with them other than at the funeral, or it may mean attending the funeral with them.

If you have maintained contact with your ex-spouse and his family, you should call at the funeral home and write a condolence note to your former partner's closest relatives. If you know that everyone, including the present spouse, will be comfortable with your presence, you may even attend the funeral—but if you do, don't impose yourself on the family by sitting with them (unless they invite you to do so) or otherwise act as if you were a primary mourner.

CHILDREN AND FUNERALS

In deciding whether to take a child to a funeral, the child's feelings should be tantamount and should dictate your behavior.

If a child wants to attend the funeral of a loved one and is in your estimation capable of handling this, then you may take him. Infants and children under the age of four or five are usually not taken to funerals because they cannot understand what is happening. But a nursing mother who has suffered a loss may have to take an infant with her. Since the mother's need (for a few days, at least) is to mourn her loss, parents of such an infant may want to consider hiring someone to help them with the baby or small child at the funeral home, during the service, and immediately afterward. This way, baby can be brought to the mother when she needs to nurse and taken away when she starts to fuss.

LOSS OF A PET

The loss of a pet who has been part of one's life for a long time can be devastating—almost as devastating as the loss of a human.

Pets usually are not buried in a religious ceremony—some religions even oppose this—but if you feel the need, you can arrange some small ceremony to comfort you. Your veterinarian can advise you about pet burials.

It is appropriate and kind to offer condolences to someone who has lost a beloved pet. Again, you don't have to say much; just let the person know that you understand and are sorry for their loss. And as is the case when a human companion has been lost, a little extra, tactful attention at this time is greatly appreciated.

———

ALTHOUGH WE HAVE FAR FEWER RULES THAN WE USED TO about dealing with loss, many people still worry that they won't behave the right way or, worse, say the right thing to someone who has suffered a loss. So despite the best of intentions, they end up doing nothing. They say nothing, they don't pay a call, they don't send a note.

There is no need for anyone to feel hesitant about responding to another's loss. As long as we truly feel for the other person, there isn't much that we can do or say that will give offense. Well-meaning sympathy, however awkwardly put (and it is rarely as awkward as we imagine it is), is always better than none and is much needed by those who have suffered a loss.

Appendix 1

BIRTHSTONES

These are the stones that are by tradition associated with each month:

January	Garnet
February	Amethyst
March	Aquamarine, bloodstone
April	Diamond
May	Emerald
June	Pearl, moonstone
July	Ruby
August	Peridot, sardonyx
September	Sapphire
October	Opal, tourmaline
November	Topaz
December	Turquoise, lapis lazuli

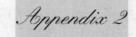

Appendix 2

TRADITIONAL ANNIVERSARY GIFTS

Following is a list of traditional presents for anniversaries:

First	Paper
Second	Cotton
Third	Leather
Fourth	Linen
Fifth	Wood
Sixth	Iron
Seventh	Copper
Eighth	Bronze
Ninth	Pottery
Tenth	Tin or aluminum
Eleventh	Steel
Twelfth	Silk
Thirteenth	Lace
Fourteenth	Ivory

Fifteenth	Crystal or glass
Twentieth	China
Twenty-fifth	Silver
Thirtieth	Pearl
Thirty-fifth	Coral or jade
Fortieth	Ruby
Forty-fifth	Sapphire
Fiftieth	Gold
Sixtieth	Diamond

Index

A
Activities, public, 124–128
Adoption announcements, 231–232
Adult children returning to family, 21–23
Adults, birthday parties for, 165–166
AIDS test, 53
American flag, displaying, 122–123
American-style eating, 186
Anniversary gifts, traditional, 281–282
Anniversary parties, 165
Announcements
    adoption, 231–232
    birth, 228–231
    death, 262–263
Answering condolence notes, 208
Appetizers, 157
Applause during performances, 126–127
Appropriate dress, 133
Artichokes, eating, 199

B
Baby, living with a, 14–15
Baby gifts, 238
Baby-sitters, 37
Baptism, 234–237
Baptismal dress, 236

Barbecues, 163
Bar or bat mitzvah, 240–242
Bathroom manners, 24
Bills, restaurant, 131–132
Birth, religious ceremonies surrounding, 234–238
Birth announcements, 228–231
Birthday parties
    for adults, 165–166
    for children, 166–167
Birthstones, 279–280
Bonus
    for employees, 93
    for household help, 38
Bores, escaping, 72–73
Bosses
    getting along with, 87–88
    good, rules for, 89–90
Bowing, polite, 69
Breakage at parties, 173
Breaking up family, 29–32
Brewing tea, 147–148
Bridal showers, 164
Bris, 234, 237–238
Brunch, 162
Buffet dinners, 143, 153–155

Buffet tables, 154–155
Building traditions in family life, 25
Burial, 271
Burial clothes, choosing, 258–259
Business correspondence, personal, 217–219
Business entertainment, 105–106
Business letters, 218–219
Business occasions, dressing up for, 99
Business stationery, 218

C

Calling customs after death, 268
Caretakers, child, 36
    gifts for, 114
Caskets, choosing, 258
Cellular telephones, 134
Ceremonies, 228–253
    religious, surrounding birth, 234–238
Chain of command, military, 224
Champagne, 160–161
Champagne glass, 180, 181
Charitable contributions or flowers, funeral,
    264–266
Children
    adult, returning to family, 21–23
    birthday parties for, 166–167
    caretakers for (see Caretakers, child)
    correspondence of, 18–19
    dining out with, 111
    family life with, 14–25
    funerals and, 277
    going out alone, 111–112
    ill, going out with, 111
    manners for, 15–18
    naming, 232–233
    privacy of, 15–16
    in public, 108–113
    in reconstituted family, 30–32
    spilling or dropping food, 193
    table manners for, 17
    teachers of, getting along with, 114–116
    teaching importance of sharing to, 17–18
    thank-you notes of, 18–19
    using titles for adults, 18
Chitchat in office, 86–87
Choking at meals, 191
Chores, domestic, 12, 13–14
Christening gowns, 236
Christenings, gifts at, 235–236
Christian confirmation, 239–240
Christmas letters, 217
Clams, eating, 196
Class distinctions, 33
Cleaning persons, 36
Clergy titles, 226–227
Cocktail parties, 144, 148–153
    drinking at, 150–152
    food at, 152
    help at, 152–153

space for, 149–150
Coffee, service for, 146
Coffee and dessert parties, 145–147
Cognac glass, 180, 181
Cohabiting couples, 55–56
Collections, office, 91–92
Commercial condolence cards, 207
Commercial greeting cards, 214–215
Communications
    in office, 103–105
    in single life, 51–52
Communion, first, 238–239
Communities (see Neighborhoods)
Complaints, 10–11
Compromises, 9
Concerts, attending, 125–126
Condolence notes, 206–207
    answering, 208
Condoms, 53–54
Confirmation
    Christian, 239–240
    Jewish, 240–242
Continental-style eating, 186, 187
Conversations
    humor in, 74
    with strangers, 69–75
Cookouts, 163
Coping with prejudice, 74–75
Correspondence, 202–227
    of children, 18–19
    handwritten, 204–209
    personal business, 217–219
Coughing
    at meals, 190–191
    during performances, 128
Co-workers
    dating, 95
    greeting, in office, 86–87
    rejection from, 96
Cremation, 271
Criticism
    of child's teacher, 115
    of employee, 35
Cutting up food, 192–193

D

Dance performances, attending, 125
Dates, meeting potential, 44–45
Dating, 47–50
    paying when, 48–49
Dating co-workers, 95
Day care centers, 36–37
Day care courtesies, 113–114
Death, 254–278
    actions after announcement of, 266–269
    calling customs after, 268
    care of body after, 259
    of ex-spouse, 276
    losing partner to, 58–61

mourning after (*see* Mourning after death)
of pets, 277
steps in handling, 254–256
woman's name after, 61
Death announcements, 262–263
Death notices, 261–262
Dessert and coffee parties, 145–147
Desserts, eating, 183
Dining out, 128–133
with children, 111
Dinner parties, 155–162
seating at, 159
table set for, 158
Dinner plates, 181–182
Dinners
buffet, 143, 153–155
glassware at, 176, 179
potluck, 162
Disagreements, 10
Discretion, 10, 94
Dishes and glasses, 144
Divorce, 29–32
losing partner to, 58–61
woman's name after, 61
Doctors, titles for, 221
Domestic chores, 12, 13–14
Dress
appropriate, 133
baptismal, 236
formal invitations and, 214
for funerals, 270
for wedding party, 248–249
Dress code, office, 97–99
Dress-down Fridays, 98–99
Dressing up for business occasions, 99
Drinking
at buffet dinners, 154
at business entertainments, 105–106
at cocktail parties, 150–152
at dinner parties, 160–161
at parties, 169–170
Dropped or spilled food, 193–194
Drugs at parties, 169

E
Eastern Orthodox services, 250–251
Eating in office, 99–101
Eating out (*see* Dining out)
Eating tricky food, 196–201
Elevator etiquette, 102–103
E-mail, 105
Employees
criticizing, 35
good, rules for, 88–89
new, welcoming, 90–91
Employers, representing, 85–86
Engagement rings, 59
Engraved stationery, 203
Entertaining, 135–174

business, 105–106
common problems with, 168–170
formal and informal, 137
for singles, 40–41
Entrée course, 157
eating, 183
Escaping bores, 72–73
Espresso, 146–147
Esq., 222
Eulogies, 261
Ex-spouse, death of, 276

F
Family
adult children returning to, 21–23
breaking up, 29–32
in-law relations in, 26–28
intermarried, 28–29
reconstituted, 30–32
telephone etiquette in, 23–24
Family finances, 14
Family life, 9–39
building traditions in, 25
with children, 14–25
purposes of, 39
turf wars in, 23–24
Faxes, 105
Finances, family, 14
Finger bowls, 189
Firing help, 34–35
First communion, 238–239
Fish course of meal, eating, 182
Fish forks, 177
Flag, American, displaying, 122–123
Flattery, 73–74
Flatware (*see* Utensils)
Flexibility, 27–28
Flowers or charitable contributions, funeral, 264–266
Food
at buffet dinners, 153–154
at cocktail parties, 152
cutting up, 192–193
for dinner parties, 156–157
new, dealing with, 201
pests in, 194
reaching for, 192
served family style or in courses, 184
sharing, 194–195
spilled or dropped, 193–194
tricky, eating, 196–201
with wine, 160–161
Formal birth announcement, 229
Formal entertaining, 137
Formal invitations, 209–212
Formality at parties, levels of, 143–145
Formal place settings, 176–178
Formal weddings, 245–246, 248–249

Friends
gifts among, 78–79
greeting, 63–67
helping friends, 80
ill, help for, 82
reciprocating with, 81
sick (*see* Sick friends)
Friendships, 63–84
ending, 83–84
maintaining, 77–79
youthful, 21
Frog's legs, eating, 200
Fruit course, eating, 183
Funeral flowers or charitable contributions,
264–266
Funeral home calls, 268–269
Funeral preparations, 255, 256–263
Funerals, 269–272
actions after, 272–274
children and, 277
dress for, 270
Jewish, 270–271
Funeral services, 260–261

G
Gay relationships, 56–57
Gifts
anniversary, traditional, 281–282
baby, 238
for caretakers, 114
for child's teacher, 116
at christenings, 235–236
for Christian confirmation, 240
for friends, 78–79
hostess, 79
for household help, 38
for lovers, 54–55
office, 93
for weddings, 247
Glasses and dishes, 144
Glassware
at dinners, 176, 179
shapes of, 180–181
Gloves, 65
Godparents, 235
Gossip, 71, 89
Government officials, titles of, 222–223
Grace, saying, 190
Graduations, 243–244
Greeting cards
commercial, 214–215
holiday, 215–216
Greeting co-workers in office, 86–87
Greeting friends, 63–67
with kissing, 65–66
Greeting new neighbors, 119–120
Guests
good, rules for, 171–173
surprise, 168–169

H
Handicapped people, helping, 133–134
Handshaking, 63–65
Handwritten correspondence, 204–209
Harassment, sexual, 97
Headings of business letters, 218–219
Heimlich maneuver, 191
Help
at buffet dinners, 155
at cocktail parties, 152–153
firing, 34–35
for friends, 80
for handicapped people, 133–134
hiring, 34
household, 32–38
for ill friends, 82
live-in, 37
overweening, 81
Herbal teas, 148
Hiring help, 34
Holiday greeting cards, 215–216
printed, 216
signing, 216
Holidays, singles and, 57–58
Honoring plans, 43
Hostess gifts, 79
Hosts, good, rules for, 170–171
Hot napkins, 189
Household help, 32–38
Households for singles, 40–41
Humor in conversation, 74

I
II, III, Jr., and Sr., 220–221
Ill children, going out with, 111
Ill friends, help for, 82
Informal entertaining, 137
Informal invitations, 213
Informal place settings, 178, 179
Informals, 203, 204
Informal weddings, 247–249
invitations to, 213
In-law relations in family, 26–28
Intermarried family, 28–29
Intimacy, singles and, 51–55
Introductions, 67–69
in new neighborhoods, 120–121
Invitations, 209–214
for buffet dinners, 153
for cocktail parties, 149
to dinner parties, 156
formal, 209–212
to graduations, 243–244
informal, 213
to informal weddings, 213
nontraditional wedding, 213–214
oral, 139–140
to party guests, 138–139
receiving, 142

responding to, 211–212
telephone, 139–140
time of, 144–145
timing of, 142–143
written, 140–141

J
Jewish confirmation, 240–242
Jewish funerals, 270–271
Jewish services, 251–252
Joint social calendars, 11
Jr., Sr., II, and III, 220–221
Just-to-be-nice notes, 208–209

K
Kissing, greeting friends with, 65–66
Kiwi fruit, eating, 200

L
Lawyers, titles for, 222
Lesbian relationships, 56–57
Letters
    business, 218–219
    Christmas, 217
Line etiquette, 124
Live-in help, 37
Living together as lovers, 55–56
Lobster, eating, 198–199
Longtime partners, 262
Losses (see Death)
Lovers
    gifts for, 54–55
    living together as, 55–56
Lunch parties, 162

M
Mail, office, 104–105
Maintaining friendships, 77–79
Mangoes, eating, 200
Manners, 7
    for children, 15–18
    function of, 7–8
    table, 175–201
Marriage, 9–14
    privacy in, 11
    social life in, 12–13
Mass cards, 266
Matchmaking, 45
Meals
    posture at, 192
    smoking at, 195–196
    starting, 189–190
Meeting potential dates, 44–45
Meeting singles, 42–50
Memorial services, 271–272
Menu (see Food)
Military titles, 224–225
Mingling with singles, 45–47
Miscarriages, 275–276

Miss, Mrs., and Ms., 220
Mothers-in-law, 26
Mourning after death, 274–275
    sending cards to those in, 216–217
Movies, attending, 125
Mrs., Miss, and Ms., 220
Muslims, 252

N
Naming ceremony, 234, 237–238
Naming children, 232–233
Napkins, using, 188–189
    hot, 189
Neighborhoods
    new, introductions in, 120–121
    volunteering in, 121–122
Neighbors
    getting along with, 116–121
    new, greeting, 119–120
    reasonable boundaries with, 118–119
Nontraditional wedding invitations, 213–214

O
Obituaries, 261–262, 263
Office
    eating in, 99–101
    smoking in, 101–102
Office chitchat, 86–87
Office collections, 91–92
Office communications, 103–105
Office dress code, 97–99
Office gifts, 93
Office greetings, 86–87
Office life, 85–107
Office mail, 104–105
Office parties, 92–93
Office romances, 94–97
Office social life, 91–93
Office telephone, 103–104
Olive oil, eating, 200
Open house parties, 163–164
Oral invitations, 139–140
Ordering wine, 129–131
Ovations, standing, 126–127
Overweening help, 81
Oysters, eating, 196

P
Pallbearers, 267–268
Paper plates, 144
Parties
    birthday (see Birthday parties)
    breakage at, 173
    cocktail (see Cocktail parties)
    dinner (see Dinner parties)
    drinking at, 169–170
    drugs at, 169–170
    guests at, invitations for, 138–139
    kinds of, 143–168

levels of formality at, 143–145
lunch, 162
office, 92–93
open house, 163–164
planning, 138–143
reasons for, 136–137
smoking at, 169–170
surprise, 167–168
tea, 147–148
throwing, 135–137
Pasta, eating, 200
Patriotism, displaying, 122–123
Paying when dating, 48–49
Performances
    applause during, 126–127
    talking during, 126
Persimmons, eating, 200–201
Personal business correspondence, 217–219
Pests in food, 194
Pets, death of, 277
Place cards, 190
Place settings, 176–182
Planning parties, 138–143
Plans, honoring, 43
Plastic utensils, 144
Plates, dinner, 181–182
Plays, attending, 125
Polite bowing, 69
Politeness, 16, 50, 134
Posture at meals, 192
Potluck dinners, 162
Prejudice, coping with, 74–75
Presents (see Gifts)
Printed holiday cards, 216
Printed stationery, 203
Privacy, 89
    of children, 15–16
    in marriage, 11
Promptness, 31, 50, 172
Protestant services, 250
Protocol, 202–227
Public, children in, 108–113
Public activities, 124–128
Public life, 108–134

R
Racial intermarriage, 28–29
Raises for household help, 38
Ramadan, 252
Reaching for food, 192
Reciprocating with friends, 81
Reconstituted family, 30–32
Rejection from co-workers, 96
Relationships
    same-sex, 56–57
    sexual, 51–55
Religious cards, 215–216
Religious ceremonies surrounding birth, 234–238

Religious intermarriage, 28–29
Religious services, 249–252
Reply cards, 212
Rescuing wallflowers, 170
Reservations, restaurant, 128
Respect, 15, 112
Responding to invitations, 211–212
Restaurant bills, 131–132
Restaurant reservations, 128
Restaurants, tipping in, 132
Restaurant seating, 128–129
Robert's Rules of Order, 121
Roman Catholic services, 250–251
Romances, office, 94–97
RSVP, 141, 210
Ruptured friendships, 83–84

S
Salad course, 157
    eating, 183
Same-sex couples, 56–57
    birth announcements from, 231
Saying grace, 190
Seafood course of meal, eating, 182
Seating
    at dinner parties, 190
    in restaurants, 128–129
Secondhand smoke, 101
Semiformal weddings, 246, 248–249
Servants, 32–38
Services
    Eastern Orthodox, 250–251
    funeral, 260–261
    Jewish, 251–252
    memorial, 271–272
    Protestant, 250
    religious, 249–252
    Roman Catholic, 250–251
Sexual etiquette, 51–55
Sexual harassment, 97
Sexual orientation, 56–57
Shaking hands, 63–65
Sharing food, 194–195
Sherry glass, 180
Shivah, sitting, 273–274
Showers, bridal, 164
Siblings, 20, 257
Sick friends
    gifts for, 82
    visiting, 83
Signing holiday cards, 216
Singles, 40–62
    birth announcements from, 230–231
    entertaining for, 40–41
    holidays and, 57–58
    households for, 40–41
    intimacy and, 51–55
    meeting people, 42–50
    mingling with, 45–47

Sit-down dinners, 155–162
Sitting shivah, 273–274
Smoke, secondhand, 101
Smoking
  at meals, 195–196
  in office, 101–102
  at parties, 169
Snails, eating, 196–197
Sneezing
  at meals, 190–191
  during performances, 128
Social calendars, joint, 11
Social life
  in marriage, 12–13
  office and, 91–93
Soup course of meal, eating, 182–183
Spilled or dropped food, 193–194
Sr., Jr., II, and III, 220–221
Standing ovations, 126–127
Starting meals, 189–190
Stationery, 202–204
  business, 218
Stillbirths, 275–276
Strangers, conversations with, 69–75
Surprise guests, 168–169
Surprise parties, 167–168

T
Table manners, 175–201
  for children, 17
  specific, 190–196
Table setting for dinner parties, 158
Taboo topics, 71, 75–77, 195
Talking during performances, 126
Tea, brewing, 147–148
Teachers of children, getting along with, 114–116
Teaching importance of sharing to children, 17–18
Tea parties, 147–148
Teenagers, living with, 19–20
Telephone etiquette in family, 23–24
Telephone invitations, 139–140
Telephones
  cellular, 134
  office, 103–104
Thank-you notes, 8, 204–206
  of children, 18–19
Throwing parties, 135–137
Timing of invitations, 142–143
Tips
  for household help, 38

  in restaurants, 132
Titles, 219–227
  for adults, children using, 18
  clergy, 226–227
  of government officials, 222–223
  military, 224–225
Topics, taboo, 71, 75–77, 195
Traditional anniversary gifts, 281–282
Traditions in family life, building, 25
Tricky food, eating, 196–201
Turf wars in family life, 23–24
TV etiquette, 24

U
Ushers, 267–268
Utensils
  American and continental eating styles with, 186–187
  placing of used, 188
  plastic, 144
  resting and done positions for, 184, 185
  rule for using, 178–179

V
Visiting sick friends, 83
Volunteering, 44, 58
  in neighborhoods, 121–122

W
Wakes, 272–273
Wallflowers, rescuing, 170
Wedding gifts, 247
Wedding invitations, nontraditional, 213–214
Wedding party, dress for, 248–249
Wedding rings, 59
Weddings, 244–249
  formal, 245–246, 248–249
  informal (see Informal weddings)
  semiformal, 246, 248–249
Wedding showers, 164
Welcoming new employees, 90–91
Wills, 257
Wine, ordering, 129–131
  with food, 160–161
Wineglass, 180
Writing paper, 202–203
Written invitations, 140–141

Y
Youthful friendships, 21